CROSSING
THE THRESHOLD

Watch for Future Book & CD Releases at:
http://www.talayahstovall.com

Coming Soon:

"Light Bulb Moments: Seeing God in Every Day Circumstances"
A compilation of inspirational messages.

For more information or to give feedback,
email: talayah@talayahstovall.com

CROSSING *the* THRESHOLD

Talayah G. Stovall

with

Valencia E. Edner

Cover design, photography and interior art by Robert Horn.
Author's photo by David O. Ringer

Published by WingSpan Press, Livermore, CA
www.wingspanpress.com

The WingSpan name, logo and colophon are the trademarks of WingSpan Publishing.

EAN: 978-1-59594-048-3
ISBN: 1-59594-048-0

Library of Congress Number: 2006922907

Dedication

To the awesome women who are in the process of becoming
sensational Door Belles – the Proverbs 31 women. Hang
in there and never give up! I hope you gain some insight
from this book that will help you in your current and future
relationships.

Acknowledgements

To God, for always being patient with me, even when I get off track. Thank You for confirmation that we were on the right track with this book.

To my mom, who thinks I should be nothing less than a world leader - thank you for always believing in my abilities and for always loving me.

To my big brothers: Ty, I think you were more excited about this book than I was. Thanks for sharing your resources and feedback. Will, thanks for your eagle editing eye. Thanks to both of you and to our dad's memory, for showing me what it means to be strong Christian men.

To my mentor, Les Brown, who has been a tremendous resource.

To Pastor J, for the inspiring teachings on "Purpose" that kept me encouraged.

To my dear friends for their encouragement and support. I'm afraid to name names for fear of leaving someone out, but you know who you are.

Special thanks to those whose brains I picked for free and who openly shared their relationship secrets with me. Sorry, no royalties will be coming your way, but I do appreciate you.

And extra special appreciation to Valencia (Vee) for the ideas we shared during the late night conversations that brought the concept into being, and for being a true friend over the past 20 years. Most friendships take time to build, but ours was instant and has been lasting!
Love you, girl!

CONTENTS

Foreword

In my life there's been heartache and pain
I don't know if I can face it again
Can't stop now, I've traveled so far
To change this lonely life

I wanna know what love is*

You may not know the song, but you definitely know the feeling. You know the feeling of loneliness that leads to endless searching. Women are often searching to find that "perfect" man; the one who will validate them and give meaning to their lives. In the process, their behavior gets in the way. Instead of showing themselves to be the "Belle" of the ball, they lay themselves down as Door Mats or expect to be uplifted as Door Prizes. The problem is, life's meaning is not found in a man. It is revealed when we allow ourselves to be used by God. Rather than search for another individual, we must search to develop ourselves AFTER we first seek God and His kingdom.

Often in life, God wants to use us, but He must first prepare us to be used. You see, it is more than a cliché that "without a test there can be no testimony." God will allow us to experience things, and sometimes *send* us to experience things to give us a usable testimony. We face trials, not only for our learning, but so that we may be of help to someone else. In the end, it is not us who deserves the thanks and the glory, but God.

Scripture is full of everyday people who were used by God. Their lives felt meaningful when they allowed themselves to be prepared and used. Look at Moses, a shepherd and murderer used to lead Israel out of bondage and into the Promised Land. Hannah was an ordinary housewife chosen to be the mother of Samuel. God prepared David, a shepherd boy, to be the greatest king that ever lived. And last, but not least, a peasant girl by the name of Mary was chosen and prepared to be the mother of the Christ. Each of them had to face adversity, tests, and trials in order to be used by God.

This is a lesson that both Talayah Stovall and Valencia Edner have learned. These powerful women of God have also had their share of relationship experiences. Stovall is an author, certified trainer and motivational speaker, trained by my friend and mentor, "The Motivator", Les Brown. She admits to having had a few "Door Prize tendencies" in the past, but is thoroughly committed to achieving "Door Belle" status. Formerly married but currently divorced, Rev. Edner knows firsthand about the "perils of Door Mat living," and welcomes the opportunity to share the insights and wisdom of her experiences in order to make a difference in the lives of others. These women recognized that they were being prepared for a time such as this; a time to share their testimonies. Because they are willing to share their experiences and the experiences of women universally, these testimonies can save more than just your relationship. They can save your life.

God wants to use you. He allows you to go "through" so that He can bring you "to". What is God bringing you "to"? Is it a greater sense of self worth? A healthy relationship? A stronger marriage? Are you ready to receive it? What must you go "through" to get there? And once your struggle ends, what will be your testimony? What lessons will you learn that you can share with others on a similar journey? How will you help them see God in all of His glory?

Crossing the Threshold: Opening Your Door to Successful Relationships will help you develop an understanding of who you are so that you can grow into the woman that God designed you to be. The women mentioned in these pages are not the only ones to experience the hardships of being a Door Mat or a Door Prize. This is *your* story; *my* story. This is the story of thousands of silent voices yearning to cross the threshold and open the door.

Linda G. Owens, Ph.D.
Relationship Coach
www.Drlindaowens.com

* Lyrics from the song *I Want to Know What Love Is* by Foreigner

Introduction

I am not a soap opera fan, but I just happened to turn on the television the other day and Erica Kane was getting married —again! Someone mentioned that this was number six! She was, once more, promising to love and cherish until death did they part. Well, this time she took her new husband's last name, unlike when she married his brother a few years ago, so perhaps she plans on keeping it. Erica is probably not so different from many of us in real life-we just don't go through all the ceremonies. How is it that we can try so hard to find a lasting relationship and never seem to get it right?

It is commonly accepted that people will prepare themselves for a lifelong career. We go to school to get an education which will make us successful in our chosen endeavors. We take workshops and read books to hone our business skills in the arena of our choice so that current and prospective employers will consider us worthy. As technology changes, we quickly learn new systems to keep ourselves marketable. Entrepreneurs work even more diligently to make their businesses successful. We spare no expense, when it comes to time or money, to prepare ourselves for "the future".

However, when it comes to preparation for a lifetime of matrimony, we expect things to fall into place naturally. We want those we date and the lucky person we marry to take us as we are. How many times have you heard someone say, "This is just the way I am. If they don't like it, they can move on," or "He (or she) had better accept me as I am."? Why is it acceptable to invest years of time and thousands of dollars to prepare ourselves for a career which will last us only until retirement, but not for a relationship that should last us the rest of our lives? Most people think it is a waste of time to read books or attend workshops that will help them build the skills necessary to have a successful relationship. Consider this: anything worth having—a career or a relationship—is worth working for and on. And most of us, present company included, did not just come with all of the skills inherently present. We can save years of unhappiness and unfruitful relationships by simply taking the time to prepare ourselves for Mr. or Ms. Right by *being* Mr. or Ms. Right.

This book is written from a woman's point of view, so it may seem a bit unbalanced, but the principles apply to both genders. Using "door" analogies, it examines the many mindsets in dating that cause women to leave relationship after relationship, feeling unhappy and unfulfilled and generally believing that it is "the other person's fault." The intent is to help you to discover the person you were truly meant to be. We are all works in progress (the author included), working toward being the "Door Belle". *Crossing the Threshold* addresses the process of continuous personal growth. It is not about perfection, but about coming to center and being the best person we can be. This will help us to improve all of our relationships, romantic or otherwise.

We will begin by defining who we are dealing with—a raw, unfinished door that is slightly off its hinges. We'll examine the two extreme "doors" in the dating spectrum—the "Door Mat" and the "Door Prize" —along with the many "doors" that fall between. Then, our home improvement process will take us through construction to the finished product—the "Door Belle". At the end of each chapter, there are door hooks— concepts to hang your thoughts on as you progress toward becoming the "Belle".

I hope you enjoy it and, please, feel free to send your feedback to talayah@talayahstovall.com. Thank you for your purchase of this book.

CROSSING THE THRESHOLD:

Opening Your Door to Successful Relationships

PART ONE

Defining the Doors

Chapter One

Ms. Door Mat

You've heard of her. She is the famous entertainer who stays with a physically abusive man. She is the professional woman who remains in a relationship with a man who insults her and makes her feel unworthy of love. She is the attractive single woman who will date married men rather than be alone. Maybe you'd recognize her as the woman with the downcast eyes who will sacrifice her own needs to please her man. Her smile never quite reaches the eyes.

Although she may be a superstar in her own right, this lady suffers from low self-esteem. She continuously puts herself dead last in relationships because she feels that this is what she needs to do to keep a man. She will cook for him, clean for him, run his errands, and give him money–whatever it takes to keep him happy and in her arms. She'll turn a blind eye when all signals indicate that he has other women (or other substances) in his life. Many Door Mats believe that all they have to offer a man is their bodies.

She doesn't respect and honor herself enough to wait for the right man, so although her dating card has been full-of losers, mostly–she's not married. Because she feels she is "in a pinch," she will choose a man "off the rack" rather than wait for the designer couture man that God has for her.

Being a door mat has little to do with looks (or even with gender, because a man can be a doormat as easily as a woman). It has much more to do with self esteem. A woman can look like Queen Nefertiti or a movie star, but if she does not view herself as worthy of love, or if she is convinced that she is not attractive, she may fall victim to the low self-esteem demon. She is never quite good enough to herself, so she accepts the less than queenly treatment she receives from any significant-or insignificant-other.

She becomes content with a man who is "breath and britches" as long as he pays her some attention. She tries to be everything she thinks he wants in a woman, and will go to great lengths to make sure that some semblance of man stays in her life, even if he brings nothing to the table. She is very sensitive about her looks and is willing to change them to suit her man's fancy. She'll lose weight, gain weight, cut or grow her hair, etc., to please him.

"Patrick" discussed one woman who was "so much" in love with him even though he had warned her not to fall in love with him. She would buy his groceries and deliver them to his house. She would allow him to drop by her house unannounced–with friends. But, she "got her feelings hurt" when she once tried to drop in on him unannounced. (Ladies, watch out when there is a double standard.) It turned out that he had another woman at his house when she dropped by. She retaliated by taking the circuit breaker out of his air conditioning unit, but later brought it back. They first fought about the other woman, and then ended up in bed together. This is a classic example of a woman who extended herself to the point that she was willing to accept being treated badly–even to having another woman flaunted in her face.

No one will treat you with any more respect than you treat yourself. If you show that you do not value yourself, others will not value you either. Do not let lust, love or desperation cause you to compromise your vision of who and Whose you are. Until you see yourself as a person deserving to be treated with honor and dignity, you will constantly feel the footsteps of those whom you let walk all over you.

According to "Daniel," Door Mat women suffer from "weak woman syndrome." He felt that a woman he once dated had a passive outlook in the relationship, although she was aggressive in her other life goals. She was a nice person, fun to be with and open-minded. However, she never voiced her own thoughts and opinions and never said "No." He estimated that, in an hour-long conversation, she might contribute two minutes. He wanted their discussions to be an open dialogue with plenty of give and take. When pressed about it, she would say that she was "listening to everything he said." This bored Daniel who said that her attitude also translated to other areas of their relationship. She had trouble making decisions, and instead of engaged dialogue, he got responses like, "Whatever you want." After less than a year, Daniel was ready to move on.

In college, "Carolyn" dated a guy who cheated on her and broke up with her. A charming, attractive and vivacious young lady, she was president of her sorority and voted "Most Beautiful." Keith was one of the smarter young men on campus, president of his fraternity and voted "Most Handsome." It seemed like a great match; however, Carolyn indicated that Keith made her feel as if she was insane. He would cheat, lie, kick her out of the house, and so on. She found out about another woman, who he insisted was "just a friend," but who seemed otherwise. Carolyn would still call him, wanting to be with him. They broke up and got back together again repeatedly for over three years. Even after all of this, she still felt that he was "The One" for her. They both moved to another city where they tried to renew their relationship. Then, Carolyn found out that the same "friend" had come to the new city to visit him for an entire week. Although Keith still calls and tries to get back together with her, Carolyn has realized that this relationship was detrimental to her and has moved on.

A Door Mat woman is persistently available to the man of her focus. She will wait for him to return her affections, and will call, go by his home, work or other places just to garner his attention. Similar to the words of a '70's song, "Though you don't call anymore, I sit and wait in vain . . . I'm gonna knock on your door, rap on your windowpane . . . 'Til you come back to me, that's what I'm gonna do." The Door Mat's life is controlled by her need to "fill the void."

"Terry" told of a woman he had dated who tried extremely hard to be "The One" for him. "Janice" was a very likeable woman and attractive, and although he thought she was very nice, she lacked some of the qualities he was looking for in a wife. It was obvious to everyone but her that their feelings for each other were not the same. The more he pulled away, the harder she tried to win his affections. She would go to his house and mow his lawn. She would wash both his cars. She would clean his house. She would pick him up at work, take him to her house, where she had prepared lunch, and then drive him back to work after they had eaten. She left her bicycle at his house for their rides together and said nothing when she noticed that the bike had been damaged (he had allowed another woman to use it to go riding with him). After he was engaged to be married, she still called him and tried to lure him to her house by playing the "weak female" who needed a strong man to help with a household task. All of this is desperate, Door Mat behavior. And none of it helped. If she had been "The One," that is, if she had possessed the qualities he was looking for and would have been his "match," she would not have had to do any of those things to get his attention. The innate qualities that she already possessed would have been enough. Sometimes the person you think is Mr. Right (or Ms. Right, gentlemen) is Mr. or Ms. Wrong-For-You. No amount of manipulation or over-availability will change this fact.

Another Door Mat behavior is to allow another person (male or female, boyfriend, parent, etc.) to totally control your life. Some women will not spend time with their friends or family, because their boyfriend "does not allow" them to do so. They will check in constantly via cell phone to report their every move in order to avoid angering him. A recent episode of "Oprah" featured a woman who had her face shot off by her controlling and violent boyfriend. The man ended up killing the woman's mother. It was a very sad reality for a woman who seemed to be very sweet and giving. Ladies, please recognize the possible consequences when you date a man with these qualities.

Often being a Door Mat is a generational thing. There is often a family history of this behavior that includes mothers, grandmothers, sisters and aunts. "Gloria's" family history included a mother who was in an emotionally abusive marriage with her father. From the time that Gloria was in eighth grade, her mother threatened to leave her father. She did not actually leave the relationship until after Gloria had graduated from college. Gloria vowed that she would never end up in a relationship like her mother's. Unfortunately, Gloria, a very attractive, sweet and engaging woman ended up in a relationship for several years with "Mark," who was verbally abusive and controlling. The first year, things were good. During the second year, things began to get rocky. It went downhill from there. Gloria felt like nothing she ever did was good enough. "It was either too long or too short," she explained. She tried everything to appease him, but nothing ever worked for long. She explained that this relationship was the first in which she gave 200% to make things worked because she really cared for Mark.

Mark claimed to be a Christian and was a minister at the church that Gloria attended. He was also an attorney by profession, in private practice which, in his case, translated to "no money." Gloria was, and is, a dedicated church worker and Sunday School student. On paper, his "status" at the church and in the community should have made him a good match for Gloria.

Gloria admitted that her self-esteem took quite a beating during that relationship as he made everything seem like her fault. He would tell her that she just did not know how to treat a man. He would try to use religion to control her, even though he was anything but living up to its principles. Whenever it seemed that she was rebuilding her self esteem, he would find a way to use the Bible to "punish" her.

He told her that she was a "carnal Christian" and insisted that she give up her friends because they–all Christian women who enjoyed dinners, shopping and outdoor activities together–were too "worldly" and thus unsuitable for her to interact with. She did so temporarily. But, he soon broke up with her again. She wisely decided that cutting off her friends was not an option that she could afford. Unwisely, she would still often cancel activities with her friends when the relationship was "on." Mark would break up with Gloria regularly for any pretend infraction, and she would take him back every time. Gloria stated that he broke up with her at least 25 times during the relationship.

The first breakup was over a trip she took with the "girls." He was angry because she was going away with her friends. He took her to the airport, but refused to speak to her during the entire ride. They did not talk until she returned from the trip. Once, she made a joke about him really enjoying his food, based on the "smacking" that he was doing. He got extremely angry and broke up with her over that comment. He once broke up with her over an entire summer, so that he could take time to get himself together and "be with the Lord." (Do you think that was really who he spent the summer with?) He broke up with her every holiday–Thanksgiving, Christmas, Easter and just before her birthday, thus eliminating the need to ever buy her a gift (even though he would accept the gifts she bought). He would find something to pick a fight about and leave in a huff. Gloria assumed, probably correctly, that he was leaving her early on those holidays so that he could spend them with someone else. He constantly kept tabs on her and once even called her mother, who lives out of town, to find out if she was, in fact, talking to her on the telephone when she had said she was.

During the relationship, they got engaged. He broke the engagement three times. During one of the broken engagements, Mark admitted to proposing to another woman, a good "friend" of his who also attended their church. He gave the other woman a ring, but then regretted his "mistake," apologized to Gloria and took the ring back from the other woman. He and Gloria got back together.

One engagement was broken just a couple of weeks before the planned ceremony. Then, just after the original date, Mark insisted that they needed to get married–the following weekend! Following her heart, Gloria agreed and the wedding took place. Gloria's mother did not even have time to make arrangements to attend. Their brief marriage ended in divorce three months later. After the first month, Mark picked a fight and pulled the (already signed by him) divorce papers out of his pocket. He pressured Gloria to sign the papers right away. He did not allow her to attend her own divorce hearing and would not even inform her of the grounds of the divorce. Wisely, she made some calls to find out the time and location of the hearing. Upon arriving at court, she talked to a clerk, who kindly got her paperwork and informed her of the grounds–repeated mental cruelty–on her part, of course!

At the end of the three months, the divorce was final. Mark had never even moved into the house–a house which he insisted they must have and which she ended up having to consistently work extra hours on her job to pay for.

Yet, the relationship continued even after the divorce, with more dating and another on again, off again engagement. During this entire period, this "man of God" insisted that they have a sexual relationship. When she tried to convince him that they should seek counseling and should not have sex because it was clouding the issues, he insisted that he would end up hating and resenting her if she refused to sleep with him. Gloria admitted that she made a mistake by "playing house" after the divorce. She allowed Mark to continue to sleep with her with no commitment. During the last two years of the relationship, they attended counseling at the church. Unfortunately, the chosen counselor was a friend of Mark's, so the counsel was not exactly free of bias.

Gloria and Mark's final breakup took place just before her birthday, because she turned the ringer off on her phone when she had a migraine. During that time, Gloria was extremely stressed, was breaking out in hives and was having migraines. In order to deal with the headache, she needed to eliminate all noise and light. When Mark finally talked to her, he insisted on knowing why her ringer was off and when her answer did not come quickly enough, he broke up with her. That was the final straw for Gloria. She never looked back. Three months after the breakup, Gloria learned that Mark was engaged to another woman. This would be his fourth marriage. As of this printing, that engagement has been called off.

Gloria believes that she has reached a turning point in her life. For the first time in 5 years, she says that she feels like herself. She is much happier and vows never to return to that relationship, or any like it, again. She will only work that hard again if someone meets her halfway.

Ms Door Mat, wake up and smell the coffee. Find your way to being the complete person you really are and realize your true worth as a woman. The difference between being a Door Mat and not being one is not about being patient, showing kindness, etc. It is about boundaries, determining what you will or will not accept in a relationship of any type, including romantic relationships, friendships or family relationships. If a relationship does not affirm you, cut your loses. Remember, nobody can walk on you if you do not lie down.

Door Hooks ¿

List any "Door Mat" behaviors you consistently display that you believe should be changed in order for you to improve your relationships.

_____

_____

_____

What advice would you give to a friend who consistently exhibits "Door Mat" behavior?

_____

_____

_____

If you find that you have slipped into "Door Mat" mode, use the following affirmation or create one of your own: "I will remember who and Whose I am and will begin the process of acknowledging my self worth. I can remain a giving person without allowing others to walk on me."

Chapter Two

Ms. Door Prize

You know her as well. She has always been the pretty one (she thinks so anyway). She has left a trail of men who just "weren't quite right…" Almost right, but not quite. She has never had to work to attract a man's attention and always has a boyfriend. Her motto is "It's all about me." She likes being put on a pedestal, but what happens when she has to climb down and be a real woman, dealing with real challenges?

Because of her success in attracting men, she has never felt the need to put forth much effort in relationships. He should just be happy to be with her, right? After all, she is the prize! Not surprisingly, she is single too. And, she is waiting for something that may already be there. She may miss her blessing while peering through her microscope for faults. Like the Door Mat, being a Door Prize is not restricted to the female gender, but will be discussed in those terms for the purposes of this book.

The Bible warns us "not to think of yourselves more highly than you ought." (Romans 12:3b) Yet, Ms. Door Prize will rule out a man based on looks, height, salary, etc., without taking the time to get to know him for who he is. She will decide up front that his flaws make him an unsuitable candidate for being her mate.

She definitely has the traditional "Diva" mentality. She wants her man to become integrated into her world and to be everything she needs in a man. On the other hand, she feels that her just being the woman that she is, should be sufficient for all of his needs.

The Door Prize does not intend to live a life that is ordinary. That might be good for other people, but not for her. If life were a bell curve, she would have to be in the six sigma range and leave "normalcy" to everyone else. She believes that she deserves only the best that life has to offer, and that includes the best mate. She expects to be treated a certain way by a certain type of man. She expects her significant other to live up to the expectations that she has of him regarding his appearance, career potential and personal habits more because of how it impacts her than him. She wants him operating at 100% of his potential in all areas and at all times, not because she believes it will make him happier and more fulfilled—he might already be happy, but because it fits the ideal of what she expects in a relationship (again, "It's all about me"). With her, it is not, "I love you, accept you and want you to be happy (however that comes about)," but instead "If you make me happy (by living your life up to my expectations), I'll love and accept you." She believes that people expect certain things from her and the type of mate she should have is part of that image that she is determined to live up to. Her expectations of a relationship are not always realistic. She becomes frustrated when those high expectations are not met and is ready to dismiss her man and move on to the next one, who will better fit her standards. She does not accept that the "perfect man" does not exist. After all, she is perfect, so there must be a perfect male counterpart, right? Any weaknesses or problems in the relationship are never due to any shortcoming on her part. Any relationship that does not work out is always due to something her significant other was or was not or something he did or did not do.

Like Ms. Door Mat, having a Door Prize mentality has nothing to do with looks. She might or might not be pretty in the typical sense; however, she is very conscious of her appearance. She is a sharp dresser and is always perfectly coiffed. She projects the image of "having it all together." But, surprisingly, Ms. Door Prize also suffers from low self esteem. Her quest for the perfect mate is due to the fact that she believes that she needs a perfect man to feel complete. She wants a perfect life and will settle for nothing less. But, rather than working on becoming the best person she can be and creating her own Nirvana, she searches for that perfection to come through someone else. Ms. Door Prize has the intelligence and capabilities to gain any type of success she wants, but often relies on her looks and her charm to get others to do her bidding.

This woman is used to getting whatever she wants. She often has a high-powered job or is an entrepreneur. She might hold an advanced degree. She might have a minimum wage job and still live at home, but she is still used to having control over her life. She is used to making decisions and having things as she wants them. So, why wouldn't she be able to easily have any man she chooses?

Some Door Prizes have an attribute–long hair, a striking face or physique, an Ivy League education–which they recognize as being superior to most other women. This particular type of Door Prize will play up that one attribute as her way of gaining a man's interest. She expects a man to be impressed by, and to focus on, that attribute and overlook any flaws in her character.

"Andrew" describes this type of woman as being constantly in need of attention and of validation of her looks. He declares that some will dress provocatively and brag about the many men who approach them. One woman that he knew would always let him know how many men tried to talk to her when she was out alone. He believes that despite their looks, intelligence and career status, there are a lot of troubled women out there whose egos overcompensate for the fact that they are lonely. Though they seem to have it all together, they are desperate in their own way.

"Terry" told the story of a woman that he once dated who had very high expectations of the men she dated. "Denise" was insulted that her previous boyfriend had asked, "What do you bring to the table?" At first, Terry did not understand why anyone would ask this beautiful woman a question like that but, over time, he began to agree. Although she was beautiful on the outside, she was shallow and devoid of character. She still had a boyfriend when Terry met her and, on one occasion, told Terry that she had told her boyfriend she had to go to church in order to spend time with Terry. That should have been a red flag for Terry! Denise was exhibiting her character flaws without even realizing it. The final straw became when she told him that she had to go out of town one weekend and he saw her walking around, in town mind you, with another man. She tried a second lie to cover up the first lie, but the jig was up. She was a great arm piece, but she was definitely not wife material.

Sometimes, a Door Prize might occasionally exhibit Door Mat behavior for a limited time when there is a specific man on whom she has set her sights. Something about that particular man "has her nose wide open." She will do anything to get him. She will try to say and do all the right things. He might wonder whether she is actually as nice as she seems or if she is just doing certain things to get what she wants. In the end, her true character will emerge and he will find out what he is really dealing with.

Terry cited a woman he had dated who was very sweet and giving in the beginning of the relationship but, as time went on, her true personality began to show and he saw a woman who was very hot-tempered and self-absorbed.

"Mitchell" dated a woman who was very attractive, had a great figure, was very social, talented and skilled, but very selfish. He observed certain habits of hers, like wearing a pair of shoes and returning them, and he made mental notes of behaviors such as that. She never wanted to treat him to anything, but let him pay for everything. According to him, she broke all the rules of dealing with men. She was very flirtatious and touchy with other men. He did not trust her and felt that it was always "about her." The killer for that relationship was when she came over to his house for Monday night football. He likes to cook, so he did. She brought a bottle of champagne. She came in and kissed him on the cheek. She poured herself a glass of champagne (did not pour him one), sat in "his" chair, kicked the ottoman over, put her feet up and changed the channel away from the game to a nighttime soap. At that point, he knew that he was "done." He dumped her the next morning (note the timing on that, ladies). He told her that she was not marriage material. He runs into her occasionally and, although she is now married, he says that he never sees her husband with her. And, she is still flirtatious with the men.

Another woman Mitchell dated lived in Ohio. She was a "Prize" and never realized that she was not the only one. He would see her in Ohio on the weekends and they would argue every weekend. He described her as being very moody and having a sharp tongue. She tried to convince him to let her move to Chicago to be with him, but he was not interested.

Andrew stated that most of the women he runs into are "high-powered." He discussed an investment banker who thought everyone should "lie down at her feet." At first, she seemed to be very nice, giving and concerned about all of humanity. He soon realized that "all of humanity" just included her. A dual personality began to appear. When he did not cooperate with her wishes, she told him that she could have been dating a Harvard MBA instead of "wasting time" with him.

Andrew admitted to being adept at getting women to loosen up and talk about themselves and their past relationships. Often, they would inadvertently give away their own Door Prize behavior. He claims that by playing to the Door Prizes' egos and talking about their favorite subjects–themselves, he got them to open up and reveal things about themselves. He would "trick" them into telling him how they "got" the men they dated in the past. He would get them to unknowingly "uncover their own schemes."

A Door Prize often has unreasonably high expectations of her partner. She might nag her boyfriend to change careers because it suits her image of the person she should be dating. He might be perfectly happy and content being a street sweeper, but she believes that he can and should be a stock broker. She will harass him and make him miserable because he will not live up to the expectations that she has for him. It is more important to her that his choice of vocation pleases her than that it pleases him because, as we discussed earlier, it is all about her anyway. She cannot accept her man for who he is, but will not leave him alone and let him be happy being who he is with someone who will appreciate his other qualities. The 1969 Rolling Stones hit, "You Can't Always Get What You Want," holds no meaning for her at all.

"Tony" dated a woman who thought she was "all that and a bag of chips." She expected him to do everything for her. He helped her move to the city where he was living. He got her a job, cleaned her car, and paid her bills. "It was always 'gimme, gimme, gimme'." In retrospect, he considers her a "gold-digger." He respected her and they were never intimate, however, he longed for some show of affection. She was unwilling to even give him a hug or kiss. He estimated that during their two-year relationship, they kissed about three times. They became engaged. At one point, he got laid off and needed a place to stay. Although she allowed him to pay her bills, she would not allow him temporary refuge. So, he stayed in a hotel for seven months. They broke up and he continued to pay her bills for the next two months. After the breakup, she sent him a bill for "expenses." He, in turn, showed her a record of everything he had paid and they were done. Door Prize meets Door Mat. But, in this case, the Door Mat wised up.

If a person, male or female, only cares about his or her own needs and desires and is not willing to put forth extra effort toward the happiness of others–if their mentality is "I won't do any more for you or give any more to you than you will for me," they should probably do the world a favor and remain single. A relationship will never be totally balanced or equal.

At any given time, one person is giving more than the other, but both should strive to be more giving. People who insist on perfection in others will never be happy with any marital situation. They will be frustrated and unhappy because things are not exactly as they would have them and they will end up making their partner miserable as well.

Door Hooks ¿

List any "Door Prize" behaviors you consistently display that you believe should be changed in order for you to improve your relationships.

_____

_____

_____

What advice would you give to a friend who consistently exhibits "Door Prize" behavior?

_____

_____

_____

If you find that you have slipped into "Door Prize" mode, use the following affirmation or create one of your own: "I will remember to stay grounded and focused on what is really important in life. I will relate to others from a viewpoint of open-mindedness and compassion rather than self-centeredness."

Chapter Three

Door Mat vs. Door Prize Responses

Ms. Door Mat and Ms. Door Prize are at opposite ends of the spectrum. If we were to look inside both of their brains, to analyze their thoughts, we might see something like this:

Door Mat	*Door Prize*
I'll bake him a cake so that he'll know how good a cook I am. Surely that will make him want to be with me. The way to a man's heart *is* through his stomach, right?	Bake him a cake?! Why? Is it his birthday?
I'll come over and clean for him so that he'll see what a good wife I'll make.	Clean his house! Humph! I don't *think* so. He'd better be cleaning mine.
I know that he is seeing that other woman, but I'll be so good to him that he'll forget all about her.	Another woman?! Yeah, right. When he's got all this?!
It is alright if he says negative things about me in front of others; I know that he doesn't mean it.	No man is going to talk to *me* that way! He must not know who he's dealing with.
Maybe guys would like me better if I lost weight.	They'd better accept me as I am. I'm not changing for anyone!
I've never loved anyone the way I love him.	Love!? As long as he keeps paying the bills, who needs to be in love?

The appropriate responses to these situations would not be at either extreme as the Door Mat and Door Prize responses above. In a balanced relationship, there is give and take and each person is willing to extend themselves to do things for each other, not to impress the other person but because they care about the other person. In a healthy relationship, each person cares about the other for who they are and they treat each other with love and respect.

Door Hooks ¿

Considering that balance is key to any relationship, do your responses to situations resemble either of the aforementioned extremes? If so, what would be some more appropriate responses?

_____

_____

_____

Can you think of any other situations that would reflect a healthy balance of give and take in a relationship?

_____

_____

_____

If you find that you tend to one of the extremes, use the following affirmation or create one of your own: "I will endeavor to be more centered in my responses to others. I will balance my own wants and needs with those of the people I care about."

Chapter Four

What Kind of Door Are You?

There are various degrees of "mat-ism" and "prize-ism," but they do not complete the spectrum. In addition to Ms. Door Prize and Ms. Door Mat, there are several other types of Doors that lay along the continuum. The ultimate Door will be discussed in the next chapter. Meanwhile, here are some of Ms. Door Prize and Ms. Door Mat's relatives:

- ❖ Ms. Door Post: the quintessential mediator. The "post-it" girl who is the go-between and serves as a matchmaker, but never finds her own match. She always knows someone who she can "hook you up" with, but never has a man herself. Yes, she's the ultimate note passer. She's very popular with women and men alike, yet she tends to be viewed by men as a "buddy" and not a potential mate.
- ❖ Ms. Door Keeper: also known as a "blocker." She doesn't have a man, but is quick to evaluate and give negative feedback on yours. Her comments are most likely fueled by jealousy, either of the fact that you have a man and she does not or of the time that you now spend with your man instead of with her. She is usually a very bitter woman who will take that bitterness out on her friends. She will latch onto a man–any man–just to have someone like everyone else and not feel left out.
- ❖ Ms. Door Knob: goes through men very quickly and, like a door knob, has been touched by just about everyone. This woman also has low self-esteem and needs to have a man in her life in order to feel good about herself.

However, unlike Ms. Door Mat, Ms. Door Knob will not hang in there. She will throw in the towel if she feels unappreciated and, rather than try to convince the current man to love her, will simply move on to the next man.

❖ Ms. Door Knocker: is constantly "knocking" every relationship and every man you meet because she is unhappy about her own unsuccessful experiences with relationships. She is judgmental and close minded. She is constantly spewing negative comments about your relationship and about relationships in general because "misery loves company."

❖ Ms. Door Man: blocks another's path and turns away their possible Mr. Rights because of her own jealousies or insecurities. You may never know of her schemes because they are often done before a man even approaches you. For example, have you ever found out after the fact that a man was interested in you, but upon asking Ms. Door Man about you, she dissuaded him from talking to you by making negative comments about you? The comments were not necessarily true, but they had the needed effect and now she does not have a man and neither do you. Goal met.

❖ Ms. Door Nail: (as in "dead as a") projects no life, enthusiasm or energy, so men quickly lose interest. Dates with her are often cut short with weak excuses that they have to let their dog out or have an early meeting the next morning. Men promise to call, but seldom do. Men might date her for a while because of her looks or credentials, but her relationships tend not to go anywhere.

❖ Ms. Door Plate: this woman is the sister of Ms. Door Prize. She is all advertising. Similar to Ms. Door Prize, she is window dressing–all flash, but no substance. She may still live with her parents, but drives an expensive car–and expects her man to do the same. She has little if any savings because she spends every dime she earns on preserving her image. She makes a great arm piece, but when her dates take the time to look beneath the surface, they find very little to keep their attention.

❖ Ms. Door Sill: men step over her to get to others. Why? Does she project a "mousy" image or is it her abrasive personality? It could be that she has too much baggage, is not articulate, doesn't dress well, etc. Whatever the reason, she doesn't make a good first (or second) impression. "Claire" is very tall–over 6 feet. She projects a manly appearance, mainly due to her choice of hairstyle (an afro), an unfeminine gait and clothes that are not flattering. While all of these factors are totally within her control and she is interested in attracting men, she does nothing to change her image. As a result, she tends to be either overlooked by men or immediately cast into a "buddy" role.

❖ Ms. Door Step: she helps her man get to a higher elevation, but she still gets stepped on. Her theme song is "Stand by Your Man." At any cost. Like Ms. Door Mat, she will make her own needs secondary to those of her man in order to have him successful in his profession or personal life only to have him leave her for another woman once he has "arrived." We have seen these scenarios acted out on the big screen–remember "Waiting to Exhale" and "Diary of a Mad Black Woman"?

❖ Trap Door: a man can be in a relationship with her before he knows it. He gets sucked in by her looks and/or seductive ways. Then he finds himself sinking into the quicksand of her manipulation. Often, it is difficult for him to get out without the telltale claw marks on his back. This often leaves him suspicious of the women who succeed her in his life.

❖ Closet Door: this woman looks normal on the outside, but has all sorts of hidden secrets inside her. When you open the door to a relationship with her, you never know what is likely to come out.

❖ Revolving Door: she is the cousin of Ms. Door Knob. Man after man passes through, but none stay around.

She ushers them in and back out again when she sees that they do not meet her needs. Modern TV shows like "Sex and the City" and "Girlfriends" glamorize women who move from relationship to relationship whenever the going gets tough.

❖ Automatic Door: the consummate flirt. Every time a new man of interest is on her radar screen, the curtain comes up and the performance begins. She smiles. She flirts. She bats her eyelashes. They come running. But, they run away just as quickly when they see that her performance is not a limited-run engagement.

Ladies, there's got to be a better way! There *is* a point of balance, where self-esteem and common sense meet, where a woman understands that she can both receive and give respect and good treatment. Where two people can love, honor and respect each other and handle difficulties with grace. These Doors are well on their way:

❖ Ms. Door Stop: holds the door open for others, while helping to insure against "scrapes" when the door unexpectedly flies open. She gives sound advice to other women and provides comfort and a listening ear in times of trouble.

❖ Ms. Door Way: after she has figured out the way, she helps others to get through by shining a positive light on their paths. This woman has it together herself and is committed to providing guidance to other women.

❖ Ms. Door Opener: stands in the gap and opens the door for others by making introductions, lifting others up in prayer, being an encourager, etc.

❖ Ms. Door Hinge: she connects you, the "door," to the frame. Her comments keep you grounded and strong. She does not "nail" you to the frame but gives you the flexibility to make your own decisions while staying "attached" to provide stability.

There is one more Door who we have not discussed, who

exemplifies the ultimate in womanhood. Read on to find out about this relationship-ready woman...

Door Hooks ¿

Do you consistently display the behaviors of any of the "Doors" mentioned in this chapter? Are you giving off "vibes" that are damaging to or helpful to your friends' relationships?

_____

_____

_____

Do you have friends who exhibit any of the negative "Door" behaviors listed in this chapter? If so, how will you deal with them going forward?

_____

_____

_____

If you find that you or your friends display more negative "Door" characteristics than positive ones, use the following affirmation or create one of your own: "I will be a positive influence on others and will encourage them to give their best. I will surround myself with positive people who will also encourage me to be my best."

Chapter Five

Ms. Door Belle

So, who is this new woman who is in touch with herself and with her God? Who is this Ms. Right who is ripe for a lasting relationship? We will call her Ms. "Door Belle" for she is the belle of the ball! Her attitude provides the framework for entering an open honest "drama free" relationship. She honors herself, yet has the capacity to accept a man for who he is, not for what he is expected to do or be. She recognizes that it is a blessing to be a helpmate for the custom-made, God-fearing man that will be sent to her by the Father.

She has strong morals and values and is focused on personal growth and empowerment. She respects herself and demands respect from others. She knows how to take care of herself, and although she is not waiting for someone to take care of her, she appreciates a man who treats her well. She has gained insight both from her own experiences and from the experiences of others. She has a balanced set of life experiences, both good and bad. Her foundation is built on the good experiences; however, she has learned valuable lessons from the bad ones and has come out a stronger person for having gone through challenges.

She is the Proverbs 31 woman–she takes care of business and takes care of her home. Her man is proud of her and she always "has his back." She carries herself like the queen that she is and her man treats her that way.

She is well-rounded. She is a woman of integrity. She has an ease of manner. She has a sense of who she is and knows what she stands for. She does not need to be constantly entertained and taken to expensive places in order to be content. She is flexible enough to enjoy all types of activities from basic to upscale and can fit in with any crowd. Her presence makes people feel at ease and she is well-liked by both men and women. Her man is always proud of her in social situations because she represents him well.

To paraphrase the verses in Proverbs: She is classy, intelligent and hardworking. She is a good manager of her time and uses her talents to their fullest. She is faithful to her husband and he is to her. She thinks ahead about how she can best care for her family. She is caring and considerate of others. She gives to the poor and helps the needy. She knows both her own value and the value of the work that she does, be it as a homemaker, an employee or an entrepreneur. She makes wise purchases and spends money prudently. No one in her household has to worry about what they will eat or wear, because they know that she has everything under control. She is a strong woman, a woman of purpose. She speaks with wisdom beyond her years and her words are always kind. Her children honor her. She knows that popularity and looks fade with time, so she focuses her efforts on things with eternal significance. The fruit of her deeds attest to her character and demonstrate her worth to everyone.

"Carol" is a definite Door Belle although it took "Jason" a while to realize it. When he first met her, he did not find her attractive. He liked her, he believed she was a good person, but he was not attracted to her. In fact, he was somewhat ashamed of her looks, believing that he deserved to be with someone who was prettier (Jason had a few Door Prize tendencies himself.). But, over time he got beyond Carol's physical appearance and began to appreciate her sweetness, her charming personality, her morals and values and her loving ways. She didn't try to convince him that she was worthy of his love; she just remained herself and he soon became convinced that she was "The One." They have a very strong and loving marriage today. Character shows through. There is no need to engage in desperate behavior to win someone's favor.

Daniel, who we discussed earlier, met his Door Belle at the early age of 24. He was still in love with his ex-girlfriend and not interested in dating, but he was captivated by "Tanya's" looks. They both agreed that they were not interested in a relationship at that point, but would just be friends. As they spent more and more time together, Daniel began to realize what an interesting person Tanya was. He was intrigued by her background and by the fact that she had her own thoughts and interests apart from him. He even stated that she could be a bit opinionated and pushy, but that was OK after dating a woman who never had an opinion. He did not intend to enter into a relationship with her because she was not the "type" that he was seeking. But, the more time he spent with her, the more he began to recognize all of her good qualities and became attracted to her character, her values, her morals, her upbringing and her beliefs about her role as a woman. He had primarily dated women who were 10-20 years older than him. His Door Belle and current wife is a year younger, but exhibited many of the same characteristics of the older, more settled women. This excited him and caused him to consider that she could be the woman he would like to marry.

Terry, who we also met in previous chapters, finally met his Door Belle. "Candy" is a caring, Christian woman who he met through a Christian dating service. Although he never believed that he would marry a woman who had been married previously or who had children, Candy exemplified all of the qualities he was seeking in a woman. She was kind, patient, even-tempered and honest. In fact, her honesty was one of the qualities that convinced him that she was "The One." When she was undercharged for something at a store, her first response was to return the money. This was in comparison to "Janice," who we met in the Door Mat section, who once encouraged him to keep the extra money when he was mistakenly undercharged for something. Terry was also impressed by

Candy's commitment to her Christian faith and desire to learn. They have been happily married for almost two decades.

Patrick believes that the premise of dating is to find the one that you want to be with. But, unfortunately, he let a Door Belle slip through his fingers. He dated her for four years and felt that all the other women he had dated combined did not "have his back" as much as she did. She was unselfish, aggressive and took care of business. She dressed well and was very personable. She did not expect him to spend a lot of money on her, but expected to be treated fairly and lovingly. She was one of few women who he ever took to meet his mother. His reason for passing this Door Belle up was the fact that he felt that he loved her, but was not in love with her. Another issue was that she was two years older than him and he wanted someone with more childbearing years. I am sure some other lucky man snatched this Door Belle up quickly.

When "Jim" went through a divorce in his mid-twenties, he was convinced that he would not find anyone until he hit 40. He wasn't looking for anyone and was still recovering from his past. But then, he met "Jennifer." She was classy, friendly, even-tempered and easy to talk to. They became friends. Jim found that she was not self-absorbed or critical of others. Although there were many attractive women around, something about her stood out. He is a visionary, and she has been supportive of his dreams throughout their 20-year marriage. He believes that her aura of peace and supportive attitude make her a Door Belle. His advice concerning marriage is: "don't marry someone you can live with; marry someone you can't live without." His Door Belle's advice: "Whatever you do, make sure you have the 'ooooh factor' if you are considering marriage. When you see them, you should say, "ooooh!"

"Louis" believes that his Door Belle wife has a life of her own that is not merely a reflection of him. She was not looking for someone to complete her. He felt that she appreciated him as a person, not as a commodity–single male with a job–who could do things for her. Consequently, he does not feel that he has to live life under the pressure of having to be everything to her.

This is a mistake that many people, male and female make. We look for someone to "complete" us, when we should not be in a committed relationship until we are already complete. Instead, we should look for someone who complements and encourages us. The right mate will help to bring out the best in you and vice versa.

Mitchell tells his friends that if his marriage to "Arlene" does not work out, it would be entirely his fault. He believes that Arlene is a nice person–a better person than him. "If a $100 bill were on the floor, she'd pick it up and ask if it belonged to someone" (whereas he wouldn't ask any questions). At 51, Mitchell says that he has grown out of surface things like weight and looks. If you fundamentally like the person you are with, it will not bother you when their physical characteristics change. Once you reach your mid-thirties, most people realize that the physical will not sustain. He observed how Arlene treated him, her family and her friends over time and was impressed. He found her to be very bright and giving and gradually found himself wanting to be around her more. He got comfortable with her and developed a sense of trust. He observed that a man will spend more time with a woman if he is interested (ladies, do not buy all the "busy" talk). He admitted that she is not perfect–there might be things that he would ideally want her to have more of. But, then, he also acknowledged that she would like for him to have a "six-pack" (abdominals).

An example of her "Belleness" was evident to him when she accompanied him to a wedding. She went with the women in the wedding party–women she did not know. He did not see her for a while, but when they again crossed paths at the rehearsal dinner, Arlene was there, directing all of the activities. She had found that the bride's friends did not know what to do, so she jumped right in to coordinate everything. (Hmmm, sounds like a Proverbs 31 woman to me.) Mitchell explained that she is always like that. If she perceives a need, she jumps right in and takes care of it. To him, it is that unselfishness that allows him to totally trust her.

Other things that impressed Mitchell were that Arlene faithfully visits her parents on Sundays and reads her Bible most mornings. He had lots of other complimentary things to say about her. She is smart–much smarter than him, he says, but never feels the need to prove it; she's well educated, but not arrogant. She is giving, trusting, not judgmental and easygoing. She is hardworking and excels at whatever she does. She is consistent, not pretentious. She does not have a lot of baggage and has a sense of peace about her. He feels that they have a "connection" which enables them to listen to and support each other. They have common values, as evidenced by both of them having a desire to share their large home with victims of Hurricane Katrina, which recently devastated New Orleans.

Mitchell believes that God sent Arlene into his life. After 8-12 months of dating her, he had seen enough to know that she was a potential "Belle." He says that she is "the one"–she is a good woman and a good person. He trusts her, he "digs" her, genuinely likes her as a person and she is his best friend. He says that he honors and respects her and can always talk about how great she is. And, he says, she does not even have to work at it. He feels that she is sensitive about a slight weight gain, but it does not bother him. "I like thin women, but I love my wife." "If you ever hear of us divorcing," he states, "I guarantee that it was me who messed up." Mitchell's advice to women who are dating: listen to what he says, watch what he does, listen *and* watch over time, and see if the words and actions match.

"Todd" immediately recognized "Cindy's" Door Belle qualities. They met at a Super Bowl party. As the game went on, they kept moving closer and closer to each other in the room and eventually, there were just the two of them in one area of the room talking during halftime. They hit it off right away, exchanged information and began to date. He says it was her heart that first attracted him and he believes that she also saw his heart. He liked her smile, charm and inner beauty. She is nice, sweet and a strong Christian and he saw traits in her that were similar to his mother. "My sweetheart can take care of herself," he averred.

From the beginning, they were totally open with each other and shared everything about their pasts, their family backgrounds and their views on everything. He feels that God sent her to him at a time when he was not looking for anyone. They had differences to overcome, but Todd believes that their sharing of information helped a lot. They focused on the commonalities–love of travel and family. He believes a critical strength that they have is consistency. The "marriage has its ups and downs, but the consistency is still there." They keep the magic flowing. They still share fun and laughter. They still have "date night" which could be as simple as grocery shopping. He knows that he can depend on her to pray for him; in fact, they pray for each other. They talk constantly and are willing to do whatever the other needs.

Todd stated that he fasted and prayed for a week before making the decision to ask Cindy to marry him. He believes that you have to love a person and accept them as they are. "People change–for better or for worse. You have to adjust. For example, she asks tons of questions. It is give and take. You just have to accept it. We have good days and bad days, but we love each other." He again stresses consistency, along with communication and "keeping it fresh." In addition, "God has to be in there." All in all, he believes that Cindy is "heaven sent" and he thanks God for her. "She's everything," he stated. "She's just a jewel to me." Finally, he recalled the advice of his 96-year-old aunt, who told him "pick one you'll love forever, for she will be everything to you." And, it certainly sounds like Cindy is.

We all want to be a Door Belle, ringing in the positive vibes, but it takes commitment and preparation to get to that point. In another chapter, we will discuss the characteristics that demonstrate true love–patience, kindness, lack of jealousy and pride, thinking of others instead of always oneself, not being vindictive and other selfless behavior. It is important that we honestly examine ourselves to see if we embody these characteristics. If not, we have some work to do on ourselves before we will ever be ready to have a successful relationship with anyone else. Again, this advice is for men and women–we must give the best in order to get the best.

It takes prayer and true commitment to develop the characteristics that embody a Door Belle personality. But, it is well worth it in the end, as you will see a strengthening of all of your relationships–with family and friends as well as in your dating relationships and ultimate marriage.

It takes just as much effort to stay the course when difficult times arise. We must be committed to not looking back. Once we have become this new woman, it is important not to let anyone, including ourselves, pull us back into our old habits. As the Bible teaches, one should not put old wine in new skins, lest the wine become soured and inconsumable. We cannot mix our old habits with our new habits or the good in us will be tainted by the bad. We must stay focused and allow God to develop the "Belle" within us so that she is the epitome of class and dignity.

Door Hooks ¿

Do you consistently display the behaviors of a "Door Belle"? If not, which of the behaviors mentioned in this chapter are you willing to adopt?

_____

_____

Do you honor yourself in relationships and treat others as you would desire to be treated?

In order to strive toward "Door Belle" status, use the following affirmation or create one of your own: "Keeping God as the head of my life, I will strive to live a life of balance and to be a blessing to others."

CROSSING THE THRESHOLD:

Opening Your Door to Successful Relationships

PART TWO

The
Search
is On

Chapter Six

"Dear" Hunting

Women are always on a quest for "Mr. Right," like the search for the Holy Grail. There is constant pressure to live a "normal" life–to get married and have children. We have all heard it, "When are you getting married?" "When am I going to eat some cake?" "You're being too picky." "Don't you want to have children?" "Are you homosexual?"

The not-so-subtle suggestion is: "What's wrong with you?" "Why can't you be like everyone else?" Everything is geared towards couples and we buy right into that philosophy. Even shoes come in pairs! And, what is spaghetti without the meatballs?

Women often do not feel "whole" unless they have a man on their arm. There is the story of a young woman who, when asked why she is not married, replied, "Oh, I'm getting married on the first." "Wonderful! The first of next month?" she was queried. "No. The first chance I get." Unfortunately, many women have this mindset and, in their desperation for normalcy, grab the first guy who comes along. Some singles are so preoccupied with marriage that they are unable to concentrate on the opportunities at hand. The quest to be married becomes their one driving pursuit. And, it is no wonder with all of the conditioning women receive to seek to be married.

Many women tend to get excited as soon as they meet a new man who seems to have a few of the qualities they seek. Before you can say "bridal registry" they have rushed headlong into projections of future marital bliss. In their minds, they are already halfway down the aisle and the man they just met is standing at the altar. Ladies, pump your brakes! Take your time and get to know a man's true qualities before you get all excited. Do not get caught up in charisma and fail to look at a man's true character.

When we reach a certain age and are still single, people begin to encourage us to "wait," "trust," and "have faith." Yet, we feel cheated that something so important has been withheld from us. While we wait, we should not feel as if we are in some sort of social purgatory, waiting to experience the bliss of marriage. "Your sentence is 5 to 10, with no possibility of parole…" We are not serving time or marking time. There is a lot that can be accomplished and experienced as a single person. I have had the opportunity to become involved with various extracurricular activities, spend time with friends and explore my love of travel and of shopping, not to mention write a book. I probably would not have done most of this if I had been focused on taking care of a husband and family. I am sure there would have been other activities of value, but probably not those. But, all of that can still come later.

While we need to plan for the future, we should not spend so much time focusing on our future wedded state that we do not take advantage of what the present has to offer. Life is a process, not an event. We should focus on the entire journey, not on one single step. We need to be present in the present and embrace life fully. There is a story floating through the email system that discusses how people put their lives on hold until "after"–"after I buy a house … after I get married … after I get that promotion … after the kids go off to college. …" We can focus so much on the "after" that we miss the now.

There are definite advantages to being single. As a single person, your evening and weekend schedule might be full of activities, but they are activities of your choosing, not those which you are compelled to participate in for other people. You are not creating problems at home by being out three or four evenings during the week. Your time and your money can be used in whatever manner you choose and no one will question it. So, go ahead and buy those shoes! Learn to play the oboe. Get another degree. Take that clog dancing class. Do whatever it is that you have always wanted to do. Even if it is weird, who will question it? Make a list of the things you want to accomplish in life and get started on them.

This is a good time to focus on giving back to others. Mentor a young person or visit a senior citizen. Sow into the lives of others and you will reap a blessing. When you operate in the mode of giving of yourself to others, you will become more content as you have less and less time to focus on your own wants. Love is an action word–demonstrate it to others in your life.

Being single also teaches you to be more self-reliant. Learn how to put air in your own tires. Learn where the fuse box is. Hang your own blinds. You have to be a good steward over the life that God has already given you before he will bless you with more.

It is a pretty well-kept secret, but often married people envy the single lifestyle. They have to always report in to someone. They have to be accountable for their time and for the family money. I have had a number of married people state to me, "It's not all it's cracked up to be." Or, "Take your time."

By definition "Single" is an adjective which means, in part 1)not married 2)unaccompanied by others 3)consisting of a separate, unique whole …" There is a saying that, "one is the loneliest number." But, there is a difference between being single and being alone. Marriage is not the only alternative to being single. There is no need to be alone when you can develop friendships that can be like family. For example, I know a group of people who are all transplants to the Chicago area. They all live in suburban Oak Park and spend time together at outdoor movies, picnics and so on. On holidays, they hold their own "family" dinners or cookouts. They have become each others' surrogate family and think of each other that way. We all need to love and be loved, but that love can come from a variety of sources. You can get the support, encouragement and acceptance you are seeking by spending time with close friends. And, it is good practice for marriage because if you cannot maintain quality friendships, with their challenges, how can you maintain a solid relationship with a person 24 hours a day, 7 days a week? Through friendships, we learn to practice the characteristics needed for marriage–communication, patience, sympathy, listening skills, loyalty, caring about another person's needs, etc. Through friendships we learn to love other people that we were not born related to. All of this helps us to be prepared for the day we say "I do." Although we generally think we are, we are never totally prepared for the unexpected problems of blending a life with another distinct personality or of the unanticipated pleasures that will also arise.

Some women look at marriage as being some sort of Nirvana. Being married will not solve all your problems or relieve all the pressures of life. It is not a solution to a problem. In fact, it creates issues, conflicts and tensions which must be adjusted to and overcome if the marriage is to be successful. It takes work to keep a marriage together, so while you are still single, rest up for the task ahead and enjoy the simple life. It will never be this simple again. Most children who are in a hurry to grow up so that they can do whatever they want soon find out that having a job, bills and responsibilities is not the fun ride they expected it to be. Likewise, most single people who get married soon find that it is not constant passion and pleasure, but a lot of hard work. There was a woman who was a member of the church where I grew up. Prior to getting married in her late 30's, she had struggled financially most of her life. She saw her upcoming marriage as an end to all of her struggles. She anticipated no more financial struggles. She was looking forward to having that Lexus she had been dreaming of. She felt that all of her problems were about to be over and stated as much because she was about to be "Mrs. Tom Hutchinson"!

Unfortunately, "Tom" was soon laid off his job of many years, they had a baby right away, and soon there was trouble in paradise. The couple was facing significant marital problems.

People often forget that marriage is a partnership based on commitment to each other and a willingness to work together through good and bad times–and there will be bad times. It should be mutually enriching and fulfilling for both parties. When it works as designed, there is an undeniable warmth, camaraderie and "fit" that are obvious to those with whom the couple interacts.

It is true that activities are often geared toward couples. Sometimes, it seems that the entire world is paired off and we are left alone. Though we may be welcomed by others, we feel like a misfit. We are often the only single person at family or work gatherings. Although they mean no harm to us personally, people tend to invite people to participate in activities as couples. For example, I have relatives who liked to have game parties, but the parties are always for couples. I was always invited, along with whomever I was dating. On one occasion, I was very hurt to find out that they had hosted a game party, and had not only not invited me, but had not even let on that it was happening because I did not have a boyfriend at that time. (Talk about kicking a sister when she's down…) I did not think it fair that my inclusion in playing games should be based on my relationship status. But there are times that we will feel left out. So, it is very important to have a strong network of friends to "play" with.

Paul, in I Corinthians 7:25-35 tells us that it is okay to be single. In fact, it has definite advantages. Our time is our own to spend in the manner we see fit. We can spend time developing ourselves and our relationship with God. When opportunities or crises arise, we can adjust our time accordingly without having to be concerned with how it affects our spouse or children.

It is time to realize that the search for Mr. Right begins with us. Whether we are a "Door Mat," accepting junk rather than waiting for our Adam or a "Door Prize," waiting for the "perfect man" while passing up good men that are in the process of becoming even better, or anywhere in between, we need to examine *ourselves* to make sure that the package we are offering to others is first rate. When Mr. Right comes along, he will not be looking for Ms. Wrong and he will pass us up or string us along if that is what he perceives us to be. So, how do we become Ms. Right? If it were simple, this would be a pamphlet instead of a book.

Becoming Ms. Right begins with having a solid foundation. The Bible says that a wise person builds his house upon a rock (Matthew 7:24). If you have the proper foundation yourself and build your relationship on a solid foundation, it will grow strong. It begins with knowing who you are and Whose you are. You cannot cultivate a worthwhile relationship when you are not willing to be all that God intends you to be. And, that begins with having a relationship with the Creator. When you cultivate a relationship with God first, then your concepts of self and love are reflective of Him, and consequently, you will be more prepared for a relationship with someone else.

Door Hooks ¿

Do you find that you spend a great deal of time focusing on finding and/or marrying the "right" man? Is a large portion of the conversation between you and your friends devoted to this topic?

_____

_____

_____

If you answered "yes" to the above questions, what activities can you get involved in to add more balance to your life?

_____

_____

_____

If you find that you spend an inordinate amount of time bemoaning your single state, use the following affirmation or create one of your own: "There are many positive contributions that I can make as a single person. While I am single, I will use my time and energy to be a positive influence on others."

Chapter Seven

Watch Out for the Enemy

Often, we are looking at other women as being the enemy–the ones we have to beat, but the truth is that we are often steadily sabotaging ourselves. Sometimes, the "enemy" is me. Years ago, the famous cartoonist, Walt Kelly, wrote this immortal line for his character, Pogo Possum: "We have met the enemy . . . and he is us." We sometimes turn out to be our own worst enemies–the true enemy is "inner me." Once we get rid of our self-defeating practices, we have won half the battle. To follow Sun Tzu's advice, in *The Art of War*, if you know your enemy, it allows you to outsmart and defeat him. Applying that principle, knowing ourselves (the enemy) will allow us to defeat the patterns that we have followed over and over, leading to unsuccessful relationships. As the saying goes, "if you do what you've always done, you'll get what you always got." You can not make a different dress using the same old pattern.

In order to change our patterns, we must rethink the ways we've been doing things. We must apply new standards to our lives and dating experiences. For example, some of us have been "looking for love in all the wrong places." You will not meet Mr. Right in the wrong setting. If you don't want a bar fly for a husband, don't look for men at a bar. Often, women will meet a man in these types of places and begin to date him, and then when it turns out that their man wants to hang out in bars all the time or is an alcoholic, they are surprised and disappointed. What did they expect to find in a bar if not a man who likes to go to bars? One should not expect to find gold in a coal mine.

Sometimes the problem women have is dating the wrong types of men. Women often get burned emotionally over and over because of their repeating patterns. For example, "Sarah" tends to date "players." They are exciting to be around and always show her a nice time, that is, when they have time to fit her into their schedules. Somehow, she continuously ends up disappointed. What is the problem with dating men of the playboy variety? They grow from boys to adult men, but keep their childish ways. They do not stop playing; they just change toys.

Some women are drawn to powerful men. As Henry Kissinger once stated, "Power is the ultimate aphrodisiac." However, these women often find that the powerful man they attracted lacks the sensitivity that is also important to her. Powerful men are often self-absorbed…that focus on their personal goals is how they became powerful. With many of these men–top executives, politicians, pastors–their families and significant others take a back seat to their first love…their vocations. Many have not found the balance between work and home. Be careful…relationships with these men can often be a lonely journey. The American Express card is poor company!!

We often look at wealth and success rather than looking at the man who truly loves us for who we are. We look for a man to already be all that we desire instead of one who, with our love and support, can grow to be all that God wants him to be.

Many times, we choose partners whose basic values are totally different than ours. It is critical that what is important to him matches what is important to you. Watch the signs to determine what is important to your significant other. This can keep us out of a bad situation or can help us to make a good situation better. Terry's Door Mat tried very hard to please him, but failed to recognize what was truly important to him (spirituality/church). We often focus on what we think is important to a man and what will impress him without taking the time to find out where his values really lie.

We need to destroy the negative patterns that keep us repeating the same mistakes over and over. Consider Samson, the strongest man in recorded history. Samson was gifted with strength beyond measure and had God's favor upon him so that he was able to defeat all of his enemies. He had a knack, however, for making poor choices when it came to women. He first took a wife with whom he had nothing in common because he was captivated by her looks (Judges 14) – a mistake many of us make. His parents, seeing the difficulties that he would encounter in such a marriage, tried to dissuade him. But he was determined and married her anyway. She ultimately double-crossed him and gave him up to his enemies. He prevailed in the end and went on with his life. But, he failed to learn from that experience. Just two chapters later, we see him take up with a woman named Delilah and repeat the exact same experience, not once but four times! Four times, she tricked him, and in the end he still fell for it, ultimately leading to his arrest, blinding and imprisonment. Samson was definitely a Door Mat for these two women, even to his own demise! Despite the many thousands he had fought and defeated, he was indeed his own worst enemy. A wise man said that Samson was "battle strong, but pillow weak."

Like Samson's parents, sometimes others see things that we cannot see. Proximity to a situation is often blinding. Another wise man said, "you can't see the picture if you're in the frame." If your family and friends are warning you of obvious problems which everyone seems to see except you, perhaps you need to take a closer look at the situation. Do not move forward in a damaging relationship out of fear of not having another choice or chance. Often, others have experienced what we are going through and can tell us when we are headed for disaster. We should not only learn from the bad choices that we make, but learn from the mistakes of others to avoid making them ourselves. In that way, we can move from being our own worst enemy to being our own best friend.

Door Hooks ¿

Do you have any patterns that keep you repeating the same mistakes over and over in relationships? Be honest with yourself and write down those patterns that need to be changed.

_____

_____

_____

What new patterns will you institute in order to get different results?

_____

_____

_____

If you find that you tend to get caught up in the same ineffective patterns in relationships, use the following affirmation or create one of your own: "I will stop sabotaging my own success by making the same poor choices over and over again. I will become my own best friend instead of worst enemy."

Chapter Eight

The Cinderella Syndrome

There are often deep-rooted external stimuli that re-enforce the Door Mat or Door Prize mentality. As girls, we were raised on fairy tales that told us our prince was coming to rescue us from our mediocre or unhappy lives. Said prince would ride in on his white horse and carry us off to the land of "happily ever after." The "ever after" included limitless wealth, a beautiful castle, complete with servants and a shot at one day being the queen. Not a bad deal if you can get it. And who would not love that fairy godmother?

From Cinderella to Snow White to Rapunzel, the beautiful princess never had to lift a finger, she just had to look good and wait for her prince to arrive. Many of us still suffer from The Cinderella Syndrome, awaiting our Prince Charming. The unrealistic expectations set by these fairy tales frequently follow us into maturity. We dream about the perfect wedding while failing to prepare ourselves for the actual marriage.

As children, most girls are taught to play with dolls, practicing for future motherhood. Meanwhile, most boys are learning strategy by playing with toy soldiers, learning camaraderie and teamwork through sports and learning the realities of winning and losing by racing toy cars. We are prepared for family life while they are prepared for real life. When we reach adulthood and that family does not miraculously materialize, we are often disappointed. Sometimes, our expectations are connected to the roles we saw growing up–who made the living, who took care of the household chores, who took care of the repairs, etc.

We are ready to fulfill the roles we saw our mothers perform, but who will pick up the slack?

These mindsets are often reinforced by songs, movies and television shows all the way into adulthood. R&B singer Babyface crooned, "I'll buy your clothes. I'll cook your dinner too. Soon as I get home from work." Let's see, he will bring home the bacon AND fry it up in the pan?! I can go for that. Who wouldn't?

Women love–and men hate–to watch "chick flicks." There is nothing like seeing a "happily ever after" at the end. All of our hearts beat faster when that handsome Richard Gere carried off Debra Winger at the end of "An Officer and a Gentleman," rescuing her from the doldrums of factory work and commencing a life of fancy officers' balls (how come that never happens to me…?).

Some of us envision our future to be like "Leave It to Beaver" when it could very well turn out to be more like "Good Times." We imagine the perfect couple in the perfect house with the perfect children and no problems or strife. But, that is not necessarily reality. Reality is dealing with all sorts of problems which could include finances, blended families, unsafe neighborhoods, personality clashes and so on.

Daniel believes that his cousin is a Door Prize who has a bad case of the Cinderella Syndrome. She is an attractive, professional 29-year-old woman who has never had a boyfriend. She meets men who are interested in her and goes out on dates. But, after a month-long telephone screening process, she figures out reasons to eliminate them. Daniel feels that she has a firm view of what she wants and will not date anyone until "he" comes along. He believes that her expectations of a man pursuing her and wooing her are "off-kilter." She expects that she will never have to do anything, but allow the man to buy her gifts and take care of her.

Often, we have a mental picture of the Prince Charming that we expect to marry. We make long lists of the qualities that our mate must have. As soon as we meet someone, out comes the list. Sense of humor–check. Financially stable–check. Family values–well...we'll work on that one. If we do not have enough checks on the page, we either try to change the man we are dating or we move on to the next one. Sadly, we must come to grips with the fact that the perfect man does not exist. Neither does the perfect woman. If a man were to take out the same list of qualities, how well would we rate? You will never find the perfect mate, but you can find someone who is perfect for you. Often, we spend so much time analyzing a man's flaws that we miss the character gems.

We should examine our reasons for wanting to be married. Are we looking for someone else to meet our needs? Maybe we are looking for someone to solve our problems, be they financial, emotional or physical. Much like the apostle Paul, we are looking for the "thorn" of singleness to be removed from our flesh. As God told Paul, "My grace is sufficient for you, for My power is perfected in weakness." (II Corinthians 12:9) We should not be looking to another person to provide what we feel we lack in life. God has promised to supply all of our needs (Philippians 4:19), so we should never enter into a relationship out of a sense of need.

Some true reasons for entering a marriage include: genuine love, desire for companionship and desire for a family. Additionally, there must be a willingness to commit to another person for a lifetime. If our motivation for marriage is to live "happily ever after," we are setting ourselves up for failure and disappointment. The fairy tale is not reality. Reality is two imperfect people working together to make a better life for both of them.

Door Hooks ¿

Do you have a fairy tale view of relationships and the reality of "happily ever after"?

_____

_____

_____

What mental changes do you need to make in order to have a realistic view of how a balanced relationship works?

_____

_____

_____

If you find that your expectations of relationships are "off kilter" use the following affirmation or create one of your own: "I will stop expecting Prince Charming to appear and solve all of my problems. I will take charge of my own life, future and happiness."

CROSSING THE THRESHOLD:

Opening Your Door to Successful Relationships

PART THREE

Watch Out!

Chapter Nine

Don't Be a Bag Lady

A ll of us have "stuff" that we need to throw away. Whether it is physical clutter or scars from a previous relationship, family situation, friendship, etc, all of our life experiences help to shape our attitudes and outlook on life. Unfortunately, some of our reactions to our life experiences can hold us back. We carry this "baggage" around from house to house, job to job, friendship to friendship and relationship to relationship. Different house, same clutter. Different relationship, same issues.

It is a sickness in America, especially among women. We fill our lives up with so many activities and so many belongings that we do not have room to relax and be ourselves. We are so busy with our many activities that we do not take time out for our personal needs or for God. We spend our time with organizations, family, friends and acquaintances until there is no time left for us. There are so many things that clutter up our lives and take the focus off what is really important. This baggage can take several forms:

Physical baggage: any pack rats in the house? This consists of clothes, shoes, papers, "junk." Many children who grow up with an abundance of material possessions carry that with them through life. Sometimes, having a lack of "stuff" in our youth has the same effect. We want to make up for all the things we did not have. We fill our homes with so many "things" that we have collected over the years, that there is barely room for us. These objects can become the focus of our attention and energy to the exclusion of everything else. Our minds soon become just as cluttered as our houses and we soon find that we can not focus on what we need to do to move forward in life. Not only do we not have room to develop our inner selves, but we have no room for a significant other in all of our clutter.

Mental baggage: these are attitudes that hold us back from achieving our purpose in life–feeling that we do not measure up to others, or that we do not have what it takes to succeed. Sometimes our baggage is reflective of our self concept. We often allow what others say about us or what we see in the mirror to affect what we think about ourselves. Many of our hang-ups about ourselves are manifested in the way that we react within our relationships. If we question our attractiveness, we will often assume or accuse our mate of thinking someone else is more attractive, even when he (or she, gentlemen) has given no indication that he has eyes for anyone but you. When we perceive that we are too fat, too skinny, too unattractive, not smart enough, etc, we project that concept of self to others and force them to have to carry our internal baggage. Inflicting our unresolved issues on someone else is unfair, and reveals just how "unready" we are for Mr. Right. Develop a positive self-image by listening to affirming messages, building on your positive attributes and working to improve any negative traits or issues.

Emotional baggage: this could be baggage from our parents, from past relationships or from a childhood event. We often make the significant others in our lives pay for the experiences of our past. We must keep in mind that each new person is different and should not be judged by our former interactions with others. Each new relationship brings new joys and challenges that should stand on their own. We should not let the baggage from our past affect how we respond to people in our present. For example, if a woman had an overbearing father, she should not automatically resent every man who offers her insight or advice. If a woman had a male relative who was unfaithful to his spouse, it does not mean that she should search through her man's dresser drawers for signs that he is cheating on her.

If your first boyfriend hit you (and you left him immediately, correct?), that does not mean that any man you date will be physically abusive to you. Women have baggage and men have baggage, so it is no wonder that healthy relationships are so difficult to maintain.

Spiritual baggage: fears, rituals, habits, etc., that really do not connect us to God. Sometimes certain fears or a lack of faith holds us back from being our best. We are reluctant to move out of our spiritual "comfort zone." God gave His best to us. Are we giving our best to Him and to ourselves or just giving what is left over after we have done everything else?

Human baggage: people who are space fillers or time wasters. There are people who serve no useful purpose in our lives. Some constantly involve us in extraneous activities that take our focus off what we should be doing. Others create unnecessary drama in our lives by always stirring up gossip, saying hurtful or negative things to us or being jealous or spiteful. Still others are extremely needy and cling to others in order to relieve the desperation in their lives. If they hinder your progress, aid your destruction or fail to help you reach your destination, they need to be dismissed from your life. Whether relationships or friendships, we should spend time with people who are positive, forward thinking and have our best interests at heart.

Sometimes, we lose ourselves in all of the "stuff." Between the physical, mental, emotional, spiritual and human baggage that we carry, we find ourselves crammed into whatever small space is left. We can not separate our true selves from our stuff.

In addition to dealing with our own baggage, we have to deal with the baggage that a man brings to the table, and they have to deal with our baggage. "Ben" is the youngest child, with six older sisters. He grew up seeing the "games" that his sisters played with their boyfriends. Consequently, he is immediately suspicious of the motives of women he dates. He expects them to try to control and manipulate him as his sisters did their boyfriends and husbands.

"Bill" grew up extremely close to his mother, who died over a decade ago. Sometimes family gatherings remind him of his loss. It is very difficult to deal with the loss of a loved one and, unfortunately, Bill is still mourning. Any woman he dates or marries will have to adjust to the fact that he might not join her at family functions and must accept the challenge of dealing with the void that his mother left in his life. It is no easy task to compete with a memory.

"Andrew" grew up with a different set of mother issues. His father died relatively young. His mother had mental issues and consequently was neglectful of him, treating him worse than his younger sisters. She often refused to let him eat when she fed the others and sometimes threatened him with physical harm. As a result, when visiting people's houses, he often hesitates to accept food, even when hungry. He is also very sensitive about people speaking to him with raised voices. This is something that a woman dealing with him would need to understand. Andrew was also forced to deal with some very difficult and very adult issues as a child, which caused him to have to become a responsible adult far sooner than normal. He is currently recapturing his inner "kid."

Abandonment issues can also be very difficult. "Mark's" mother left him and his siblings to be raised by their father when Mark was ten. In relationships, he began to use controlling behavior to ensure that women never left him. "Don's" father left the family during his childhood and he was raised by his mother. In the beginning of his marriage, it was very difficult for him to deal with his wife having activities that did not include him for fear of again being left.

Some people grew up with no positive reinforcement–no one complimented them when they did something well. Consequently, they may go through life thinking that nothing they do is ever good enough. Others grew up with too much positive reinforcement–they were overly praised for any small achievement. They could end up being lazy or underachievers by stopping short of their full capabilities. There are so many other examples of baggage that could be explored (health/ weight issues, poor financial management, etc.), but you get the picture.

It is important for you to identify and come to grips with your own issues as well as recognize the issues that others bring. Do not get caught up in the glitz and glamour or what looks good on paper. Just because you have certain physical characteristics or a solid bank account does not make you a quality catch. Likewise, just because a man you meet is handsome or wealthy, does not mean that he would be the best person for you to be in a relationship with.

People often change after marriage–for the worst! If you are considering being with someone but are deeply concerned about some of their habits or character traits, it is better to examine that now. Ask yourself if you would be willing to live with this man if he never changed. Ask yourself if you can love and accept him unconditionally the way he is. Likewise, look for someone who is able to deal with who you are–your positive traits as well as your faults.

What happens when we walk around loaded down with all of our "stuff"? We throw our bodies out of alignment, weigh ourselves down and slow ourselves down. There is a song by singer Erykah Badu which perfectly describes how our baggage can hurt our relationships. The song is entitled, "Bag Lady":

> *Bag lady you gon' hurt your back*
> *Dragging all them bags like that.*
> *. . . .*
> *One day all them bags gon' get in your way . . . .*
> *So pack light.*

Bag lady you gon' miss your bus
You can't hurry up
'Cause you got too much stuff
When they see you comin'
(Fellas) take off runnin'
. . . .
One day he gon' say 'you crowdin' my space . . . .'
So pack light.
. . . .
Bag lady . . . .
Let it go, let it go, let it go, let it go . . . .

At the end of the song, references are made to the various types of bags–from paper bags to shopping bags to baby bags to Gucci bags–which we carry. As is suggested by this, no matter our family or socioeconomic status, we all have some type of baggage. We need to come to grips with this, take a close look at ourselves and see if we can put any of these bags down for good. After all, we do not want to miss the bus that will carry us to our destiny.

Door Hooks ¿

What things do you tend to hold on to–clutter in your home or office, negative mindsets, negative emotions based on past experiences, negative people?

_____

_____

_____

Which of the above items will you commit to get rid of within the next 60 days?

_____

_____

_____

If you find that you are a "bag lady" (or man) use the following affirmation or create one of your own: "I will get rid of anything in my life that is extraneous or that gets in the way of my goals. I will create a mindset that is positive and focused."

Chapter Ten

Not Settling For Mr. "In the Meantime"

Do not waste time with someone who is clearly "temporary" (and we all know those who fit that description). Each of us has passed time with someone until the "right one" comes along. Sometimes, we even fool ourselves into thinking that that someone is the right one. We have all tried to shave the edges off some square pegs in order to fit them into round holes. There is something about "Mr. In the Meantime" that keeps you engaged in the relationship. It might be his kindness, his looks, his personality or his bank account or, it might be just our own desire not to be alone. But, there is also something about him that you know is a "deal breaker." So why let the relationship linger? While it is sometimes very difficult to let go of a relationship, we should never hold on to a relationship just to be in one.

Meantime relationships are used to pass time while you are still searching. But, be careful…meantime relationships still take time, and while you are spending valuable time with someone who clearly lacks the qualities you desire, just to have someone to spend time with, you might be unavailable or unaware when Mr. Right "knocks on the door." Meantime relationships are often merely filling in the emotional, and sometimes physical, gaps that are present when we seek the temporary elimination of feelings of loneliness.

Sometimes we use "Mr. In the Meantime" to help us recover from a relationship whose ending was either abrupt or particularly painful. A girlfriend of mine once remarked, "The best way to get over one man is another man." This thinking perpetuates into rebound relationships that are often more painful when they end–and they will end–than the one from which you are trying to heal. Often, women will even marry Mr. In the Meantime and will end up either unhappily married or going through the pain and difficulty of a divorce. Whenever we say goodbye to someone we love, even when we know that that person is not right for us, it hurts. We can save ourselves much heartache by recognizing and acknowledging from the beginning, that the Meantime man is not right for us, instead of trying to force a relationship. And, once we recognize and acknowledge that, we can free ourselves for a deeper love and commitment with the one who is our destiny.

Mr. In the Meantime often becomes a "band-aid" for a wounded self concept. I am reminded of a woman, "Elaine," who would cultivate relationships with clearly Meantime men in order to feel better about herself. The problem was that when she tired of their lack of compatibility, she would just dismiss the current man–sometimes without his knowledge–while she moved on to the next Mr. Meantime. While she was wasting time playing games, she missed out on a potential Mr. Right who observed her in "player mode." Be careful ladies, the singer Rockwell was right…"Someone *is* always watching you"!!!!

Do the work of learning to honor who you are, and appreciating what you have to offer. Self-actualization is an internal process, and it can not be achieved with external forces. Until we "get it" ladies, we are subject to subsequent Mr. In the Meantime experiences.

We often we fall victim to a person who appears to be "On Time," but later reveals an "In the Meantime" reality. Be cautious; being swayed by charm and style that have the appearance of authenticity, yet show definite signs of inconsistency usually means there is a façade in place. If he "looks like a duck," but acts and sounds like a dog, he is either pretending to be something other than what he appears, or he is confused. In either case, let him go. Do not hold on to hope when all the signs indicate that you should cut your losses.

The one who appears to be "On Time" could be sincere and straightforward, but might lack many of the qualities that you desire in a mate. In this case as well, the gentleman is Meantime.

Choosing a life mate is a serious decision which will impact the rest of your life. It is a decision that can make or break you. Don't settle for second best; it is not worth it in the long run. Solid relationships are built on friendship, honesty and sincerity. Proverbs 7:5 warns us to "Beware of the stranger who flatters with words." Some people will tell you what you want to hear, but their actions will reveal that they are totally insincere. It is so important to watch and listen. Women, especially, often allow feelings to overrule logic and common sense. Our intuition rarely leads us astray. If we are picking up a vibe that something is not right, usually something is not right. Pay attention to the signals.

The Bible reminds us that we will "know a tree by the fruit it bears." Mr. In the Meantime might have the looks, the money and the prestige that impress us, but he might not have the character to match. Looks, money and prestige will fade away, but character is something that does not disappear.

Some people are occupying a front row seat in your life, when they ought to be in the balcony. We need to become ushers and escort them to their appropriate place in our lives and leave room in the front row for the special person who should occupy that front row seat.

We have all had periodic Meantime experiences, and some of them were effective for our growth and our transitions in life. Meantime relationships, however, will cause problems if we fail to see them for what they really are. Acknowledge them for what they are (a friendship, a learning experience, a nightmare...) and move on. Emotions and, of course, any intimacy, should not be engaged in during Meantime situations. If he is not right for you...do not give him access to your soul. KISS....Keep It Surface Sister!!!

Door Hooks ¿

Have you ever entered into or stayed too long in a relationship that you knew was not ultimately right for you? Are you currently in such a situation?

_____

_____

_____

Make a list of the qualities that you are looking for in a mate. Use this list to evaluate your current romantic interest or keep the list in mind as you begin new relationships. (If your list is long like most of ours, feel free to use a separate sheet of paper.)

_____

_____

_____

If you find that you tend to spend time in clearly Meantime relationships, use the following affirmation or create one of your own: "I will no longer cheat myself or anyone else by spending time in relationships that are going nowhere. I will be clear on the qualities that are important to me and will not try to force a relationship where there should not be one."

Chapter Eleven

When He Does Not Belong to You

Due to what is commonly termed the "man shortage" (I do not subscribe to this principle, because I believe that God has a plan for everyone's life), some women are willing to date men who are already involved in relationships and are often even married. This is often a desperate action on the part of women who are willing to have a "piece of man" if they cannot have the full thing. They are willing to settle for a ride in a Chevy rather than owning a Lexus.

I liken this to going to a restaurant. When I get dressed up and go out to eat, I like to be seated at a table with fresh, crisp linen. I like to peruse the menu, maybe ask a question or two of the waiter, and then make my selection. After patiently waiting for a bit, I receive the hot, flavorful meal of my choice. Never would I walk into a restaurant and sit down at a table that had not been cleared of the remains of someone else's meal. Never would I eat the crumbs from another person's plate and consider that to be my meal. Most people would never do a thing like that! Why, then, is it acceptable to some women to gather up the scraps from another woman's household, i.e., her man? Why settle for leftovers when you can have a full, hot meal of your own?

Women who accept men who are already involved must deal with the constant hurt of knowing that he will never be with them on holidays. He will be with "her." The other woman will probably never get to meet the man's family. The other woman's family will not exactly be excited to have him at their family gatherings. So, when will she see him? For a few stolen hours while he is in a "meeting"? On a weekend when his wife or significant other is out of town? Is that the life anyone really wants?

Some women claim that they do not want the commitment of marriage and do not want a man around all of the time. But, even if that is the case, would you not think that they would want him around on their own terms and at significant times, not just whenever the man could squeeze them in? Would you not think they would enjoy knowing that if they made a date, the date would be kept, not cancelled at the last minute due to a "family emergency" or another "meeting"? Would you not think they would like to know that if they cooked a meal for a man, he would actually show up to enjoy it? I would!

Then, there is the issue of trust. If a man will cheat on one woman, he will cheat on another. I personally would not want the aggravation of having to wonder if, when my man is not with me, he is with another woman. That is in addition to knowing that he is with his wife most of the time. That is way too much drama for my simple life!

"Cynthia" met "Steve" while he was separated from his wife. That was her first mistake–separated is not divorced. Steve ended up getting back together with his wife because of their child. Soon, they had another child. Cynthia remained in the relationship with Steve, even though he was back with his wife "in name only." (If it was "in name only," where did the second child come from?) Many men will tell women that they are with their wives for financial reasons or for the sake of the children. What they are really doing is having their cake and eating it too. It is not your job to make a married man's life complete. You deserve to be with someone who will be committed to you. Don't ever take "sloppy seconds"!

I have been approached by married men a couple of times at various conferences. They apparently believed that I should have been flattered at their attention. Quite the contrary. I was insulted! While they thought they were complimenting my appearance, what they were really saying to me was that they did not think that I had enough going for me that I could have a man of my own. That I should just settle for what they had to offer. One told me that he was having marital problems. You know what? That is *his* problem! My life is and has always been pretty simple. Why would I want to complicate it by making someone else's problems mine?   Another man was a minister who had spoken at my church. He was married to a beautiful woman and had about four children. We recognized each other and began to talk about the church and about the conference. At one point, I mentioned that I thought it was disgusting how there were so many married men trying to pick up women. Shortly after that, he asked me who I was sharing my hotel room with. There were three of us sharing the room, and I am sure he was only thinking of my comfort when he offered me to stay in his room–with him sleeping on the couch, of course. Yeah, right. Needless to say, that was pretty much the last straw for me and I stopped attending that conference. I had made up my mind that if one more married man tried to hit on me, I was going to snap! So, rather than embarrass myself and them, I decided that I would be best off staying away.

Sometimes it is best to separate yourself from a setting or circumstance. Like Joseph with his interaction with Potiphar's wife (Genesis 39:7-12), sometimes it is best to run away from a dangerous situation. Much like the words of the 70's hit by Frankie Beverly and Maze "Running away. Leaving a bad situation..." The Bible tells us to "abstain from all appearance of evil." (Ephesians 5:3) So, if the situation looks suspicious ladies, just step away. Let married people handle their own issues and find yourself a single man who can give you his full attention.

The old saying that "half a man is better than none" has no truth to it whatsoever. You deserve better than a "piece of man." Do not make someone your significant other when you are their insignificant other. Never allow someone to become your priority while allowing yourself to be their option.

Door Hooks ¿

Has a perceived "man shortage" ever caused you to lower your standards and become involved with a man who was already attached to someone else? If so, describe the mindset you were in that allowed the situation to occur.

_____

_____

_____

If your answer to the above question was "yes," what steps will you take to ensure that the situation never occurs again?

_____

_____

_____

If you find that you are tempted to settle for a man who is committed to someone else, use the following affirmation or create one of your own: "I am worthy of a man's complete love and attention. From now on, I will honor myself by only allowing someone in my life who is free to give of himself totally."

CROSSING THE THRESHOLD:

Opening Your Door to Successful Relationships

PART FOUR

Door Construction: 101

Becoming a Door Belle

Chapter Twelve

Becoming What You Are Seeking

"If it feels good, do it!" Our modern, narcissistic society tells us that all that matters is one's personal happiness and fulfillment. It does not matter how your actions affect others as long as you are true to yourself. So, why are we still so unhappy and unfulfilled? We can never be happy when we live our lives only to please ourselves. It is in giving to others that we feel fulfilled. Likewise, we will never be in a successful relationship when all we seek is to please ourselves. We want our partner to be perfect, but we pay no attention to our own shortcomings.

A good relationship depends less on finding the right partner than on being the right partner. Most people are so focused on getting the type of mate they want that they never bother to ask themselves if *they* are the kind of potential mate that someone else might seek. People tend not to dwell as much on their own weaknesses as on the weaknesses of others. Before we seek to be coupled with anyone, we should focus on identifying and improving the areas of our own lives that need work. Quality seeks quality.

We put too much pressure on another person when we expect them to fill the gaps in our lives. We must fill those gaps ourselves, and then seek out other gap-free people to associate with. A marriage consists of two whole people who become one, not two halves that together make a whole. A relationship should never be based on co-dependency.

Being in a relationship will not "fix" the problems in your life. It will not meet all of the needs that have thus far gone unfilled.

It will not "complete" you or make your life whole. It will not make up for negative events that occurred in your life. Pray and ask God to help you deal with all of those issues. True happiness will never come from other people. It will come from within you and from having a personal relationship with God. And, what is within you will radiate outward.

We often do not have a clear picture of who we really are. There is a saying that suggests that there are three views on the matter: There is your view of who you are, there are others' views of who you are and there is the truth, which is usually somewhere in between. Sometimes we do recognize our true selves, but wear masks in order to hide the truth from others. At other times, we are so confused that we do not even know our own selves, and buy into the façade that we have constructed in our lives. In either case, the first step to improvement is recognition of the truth.

It is a good idea to query your friends and family periodically to see how you appear to others. You can ask them their opinions of your strengths and weaknesses and what makes you unique. You will often find that there are things about you that appeal to others that you never realized. You may also find that there are negative traits that you never noticed. If several people come up with the same responses, this is most likely how you come across to others. Make a conscious effort to work on the things that need improvement and to make better use of your positive attributes.

It is always helpful to have good friends, male and female, who will be honest with you regarding what you can improve about yourself, both physically and emotionally. Among some of my friends, we have a saying, when we see a woman out somewhere dressed totally inappropriately for her age or body type. The saying is, "She needs just one friend." The woman might be surrounded by a group of her so-called friends, but the meaning of the statement is that your true friends will be honest with you when they observe you doing something that reflects badly on who you are. I have a good friend who I know will tell me if I am not looking right and I will do the same for her. She'll sit me down and comb my hair if need be. I'll tell her, "That dress is not working; try something else" if need be. That honesty should also apply to any character issues or habits that you might have. If you mistreat someone, your friends should call you on it. Your true friends should offer, and you should accept, feedback on how you can grow as a person. Surround yourself with positive, spiritual people who will hold you accountable.

The Bible tells us to take the log out of our own eye before we try to get the splinter out of someone else's eye. (Matt. 7:3-5, Luke 6:41-42) We should focus on our own need for self-improvement, rather than on attempting to show another person their failings. By doing that, we not only enhance our lives, but we provide a road map for those around us to follow. What better way to get another person to improve their lives but to lead by example?

A first rate man wants a first rate woman. If you want an exceptional man in your life, you have to be an exceptional woman. Being the right person is just as important as finding the right person. Never settle for second best in what you offer or what you accept!

Door Hooks ¿

How aware are you of how you behave in relationships with others? Are you seeking qualities that you have not developed in yourself?

Is self-improvement a major focus in your life? What qualities do you see in yourself that could stand improvement?

_____

_____

_____

If you find that you typically look for more than you offer in your relationships with others, use the following affirmation or create one of your own: "I will focus on improving myself daily, in order to become the "Door Belle" woman that I am destined to be. I will not seek more from others than I am willing to offer to others."

Chapter Thirteen

Loving Yourself First

Before you can love others, you must know what love is. And, that begins with having a relationship with God and using His love as the ultimate example. In order to love someone else, you must first also be able to love and value yourself. Likewise, before others can love you, you must love yourself and recognize that you are worthy of love. If you do not appreciate and honor yourself, who will? The Bible says that we must love our neighbors as ourselves (Mark 12:31) This suggests that we must have a healthy self-love–not based on pride or arrogance, but on feeling good about who we are. This self-confidence allows us to let our guards down and be our true selves. And, that true self is the person that others will grow to love.

Our society programs us to focus on external things–looks, material possessions, etc instead of on improving our inward person. We are often so busy trying to appear as if we are worthy of love that we neglect to develop our true selves. If we spent nearly as much time trying to develop our character as we do our image, we would all be Door Belles. Proverbs 31:30a states "Favor is deceitful and beauty is vain . . . ." People frequently look at the outside of a package to determine the value of what is inside. However, we know that a priceless jewel may come in a small, plain package while a lightweight roll of fluff may come in large, colorful wrapping. But, which is more valuable: the package with the eye-catching presentation or the package with the value deep inside? Physical beauty fades with time but good character and solid values last forever. We are dressing up the outside when the real value is on the inside. It is a good thing to look attractive to others, but our real worth lies in what is in our minds, hearts and spirits. Our adorning should not be only "outward adorning." (I Peter 3:3-5) What is true and good inside of us will radiate outward. The love that we have inside of us will naturally overflow to and attract others. I challenge you to practice this on your family and friends, and see if it is true. Give unconditional love without expecting anything in return and it will come back to you.

Having a positive self-image also makes you more attractive to the opposite gender. Your self image should not be based solely on what you see in the mirror, but on what is in your character. Truthfully, physical things do play a part. If there are things about your physical being that make you uncomfortable, work on them. Proper eating and exercise can help a weight problem. Proper skin care and/or dermatology can improve a skin problem. Proper dental care can correct problems with teeth. Wear clothes that are flattering to your figure and a hair style that flatters your face. If it bothers you and it is fixable, fix it. We should do our best to look our best at all times. If you love something, you will take care of it and that means taking care of your physical, mental and emotional being. Eat right, exercise and keep your mind occupied with positive things.

Realize that you are a distinct individual, complete and different from anyone else in the world. Your uniqueness should complement that of your mate. Realistically, no person has what it takes to fulfill you. If you go into a relationship unhappy chances are you will stay that way. Happiness comes from having a healthy self-respect, being involved in worthwhile activities and having a plan for your life.

Speaking of self-respect, ladies–be sure that the object of your affections is deserving of your love and that he knows how to treat you with love. The Bible tells of the parable of the sower (Mark 4:3-32), whose seed did not take root until it was planted in the appropriate soil. Be careful where you sow your seeds of love. Do not waste the seeds of your heart on stony ground where it will not be appreciated, but will be abused and walked on. Proverbs 4:22 says "Above all else, guard your heart, for it is the wellspring of life." (NIV) Do not give yourself away to just anyone. Make sure he is worthy of your love. Remember that a man's rejection of you does not lessen your value. If a man does not appreciate what you have to offer, he is not the man for you. Move on.

Door Hooks ¿

Do you tend to focus on your external image in an attempt to mask the insecurities you feel internally? If so, explain how this manifests itself in your life.

_____

_____

_____

What unique gifts do you bring to the world that can impact others in a positive way?

_____

_____

_____

If you find that you sometimes suffer from a negative self-image, use the following affirmation or create one of your own: "I am unique and valuable in God's eyes. I have many positive and powerful gifts to offer that will touch the lives of those I meet."

Chapter Fourteen

Recognizing True Love

Ladies, if you really want to hear a steamy love story that is not on the movie screen, try the one told by Solomon, King of Israel. Harlequin Romances move over! This is racy stuff! Song of Solomon describes a relationship between King Solomon and his wife. It describes how a man and woman in love treat each other and the passion they share. His wife was his best friend as well as his lover. If a marriage is as ordained by God, he'll be your king and treat you like a queen. He will esteem you highly as Solomon did his wife and you will do likewise.

The Proverbs 31 woman, Ms. Door Belle, is worthy of an Ephesians 5 man, the ultimate "servant leader." The Bible teaches us that a man is to love his wife as he loves his own body. No one (unless he has other issues) would willingly hurt himself. So he would never hurt you, either. It is not about self-assertion, but self-sacrifice. Do you hear that, Ms. Door Mat? The right man considers your best interest to be a priority. Your happiness is as important to him as his own. The verses state that he is to nourish and cherish you. He will see you as God sees you. And, as Christ gave his life for his bride (the church), he will protect you to death. We also know that in those verses, the Bible also admonishes wives to submit to their husbands; that is, to respect his role as head of the household (don't get upset, Ms. Door Prize, just keep reading...). Yet, this scripture never states that wives are to love their husbands. But let's think about it ladies, if a guy is treating you as described in Ephesians 5, do you think you would have any problem loving him and allowing him to be the head of the family? You would be head over heels! It is a woman's nature to love those who are kind to her. These verses are really about mutual submission and cooperation–each helping to meet the needs of the other. (It is the theory of reciprocity–you treat him like a king and he treats you like a queen). The husband makes loving sacrifices for the wife and the wife respects and supports the husband in his endeavors. Both roles require unselfishness, humility and sacrifice. Each role is different, but necessary. It has nothing to do with superiority or inferiority. Men and women are equal in value, but different in purpose. If we were both the same, one of us would be redundant. We are the same in intelligence and purpose. However, we are different hormonally and physiologically. The testosterone in men makes them natural protectors and the estrogen in women makes them natural nurturers.

The verses state that he should love you as his own body. A man is typically very familiar with his own body; after all, he has had it all his life. If a man is to love you as his own body, he must also take the time to get to know you. How can he buy your favorite color flowers if he does not know what your favorite color is? How can he support you in your goals if he does not know what they are? Beware of a guy who wants to rush through a relationship right to the altar. You should both take the time to get to know each others' likes and dislikes, dreams and goals so that you can decide if your goals are in sync and if you are each willing to do what it takes to please the other.

Beware of a guy who will never put forth an effort to be a gentleman or to do things that make you feel special. Will he pump (I didn't say pay for) the gas for you at a service station… hold a door open for you…pick you up at the airport…carry a heavy package for you…send you a card or flowers…give you a compliment…really listen to you…etc? This is not to say that a man will do every one of these things all the time, but there should be some demonstration of his affection. If showing his esteem by treating you like a lady feels "unmanly" to him, remember that you can always go out with your girlfriends if you want to be treated like "one of the guys." Men who do not understand the importance of making a woman feel special do not understand the basic needs of a woman. Likewise, there are things that you should be willing to do for him to make him feel special. Men appreciate it when women do things for them like cook their favorite meal or bake something (not just when it is his birthday), help with decorating, pick them up at the airport, listen to them, treat them to an outing, etc. It is a two-way street paved with mutual giving. To quote "Andrew": "If you have a good man who does nice things for you, not doing anything to show your appreciation of him is a good way to turn him bad."

The biblical Ruth and Boaz had a relationship built on love, kindness and mutual respect. (Ruth Chapters 2-4). They made a decision to honor each other. You should treat your partner with courtesy and dignity even when you do not feel like it. As the Nike slogan reads, "Just do it!" Decide to be kind regardless of the situation. I Peter 3:7 explains that men are to treat their wives in an understanding way and to treat them with honor so that God will listen to their requests. If we honor and respect each other, we will gain God's favor. To quote a dear friend of mine: "True love always seeks the best for the object of its affection. If a man really cares for someone, he should always say, 'I want her to have what is best for her.'"

I Corinthians 13, referred to as the "Love Chapter," gives a good model of how love does and does not behave. To paraphrase the first few verses: Although one might have a command of all languages, both earthly and heavenly, if you do not have love, it is all a bunch of noise. If you can foretell the future, understand the mysteries of the earth and know absolutely everything about everything, if you have enough faith to overcome any obstacle, but do not have love, you are nothing. If you give away everything you have to the poor, if you sacrifice your very body and do not have love, it is of no value. In other words, you may be a CEO, a Pulitzer Prize-winning author, a Nobel Peace Prize-winning humanitarian, find a cure for cancer or AIDS, but if you do not treat others with love, it is all worthless.

Verses 4 through 7 list the characteristics of love:
  Love is patient,
  Love is kind,
  Love is not jealous,
  Love is not boastful,
  Love is not arrogant,
  Love does not act unbecomingly,
  Love does not seeks its own,
  Love is not easily provoked,
  Love does not take wrongs suffered into account,
  Love does not rejoice in evil things, but rejoices in the truth,
  Love bears up under strain,
  Love always believes,
  Love always hopes,
  Love always perseveres
  And, lastly,
  Love never fails. Even though everything else will fail you,
  true love never does.
  (NIV)

There is so much that could be written about each phrase in this passage of scripture that it could become an entire book in itself. Suffice it to say that we should all strive to exhibit the characteristics listed in I Corinthians 13. And, we should seek a mate who exhibits them as well.

Falling in love is the easy part of a relationship. Keeping it alive is the difficult part. To love and to keep on loving is a decision that must be made on a regular basis. In the Garden of Gethsemane, Jesus prayed that God would deliver him from his fate. He didn't have a desire to die, but he made a conscious decision to sacrifice his life motivated by his love for us. Love is an action, not just a feeling. Even if one feels they are no longer "in love" or have fallen out of love, if they have made a commitment they still must demonstrate love. Many people confuse infatuation with love and they can closely resemble each other. The chart below outlines the differences between infatuation and true love.

Infatuation vs. Love

Infatuation	Love
A Feeling	A Commitment
Based on Emotion	Based on Devotion
A "Falling" Into	A "Growing" Into
Biological	Spiritual
Admires Each Others' Strengths	Accepts Each Others' Weaknesses
Strikes Instantly	Requires Time and Commitment
Selfish	Selfless
Takes or Seeks to Get	Gives or Seeks to Share
Focused on Own Well-being	Focused on Other Person's Well-being
Holds Grudges	Keeps No Record of Wrongs, Forgives and Forgets
Speaks Gruffly When Aggravated	Speaks Kind Words Regardless of Feelings
Blind to Other's Shortcomings	Recognizes the Good and the Bad
Rationalizes Wrongs of Partner	Speaks Openly and Honestly in Moments of Controversy
Excitement/A Roller Coaster Ride	Moderate Ups and Downs
Wants Instant Gratification	Exercises Patience
Brings Up the Past	Looks Toward the Future
Tears Down and Ridicules	Builds Up and Encourages
Wants Own Way	Wants Good of the Relationship
"I Got Mine; You Get Yours" Attitude	Supportive of Separate and Common Goals
Sees Others as They Want Them to Be	Sees and Accepts Others as They Are
Focuses on Own Issues	Cares About Each Others' Problems

Together As Long As Things Are Good	Cannot Imagine Being Without Each Other
Wants Others To Fit Into Their Life	Wants to Meld Lives Together
Based on Excitement & Physical Attraction	Based on Friendship and Mutual Respect
Thinks in terms of "Me"	Thinks in Terms of "We" / Mutual Dependence
"No Romance Without Finance"	Economic Advantage is Not a Consideration
Is Possessive or Jealous	Is Not Possessive or Jealous
Talks	Listens
Tries to Impress	Is Himself or Herself
Covers Up or Rationalizes Error	Admits When Wrong
Sees Only Strengths	Recognizes Both, but Magnifies Strengths & Minimizes Weaknesses
Impressed by External Qualities	Impressed by Internal Qualities
Takes no Accountability For Injury Caused	Regrets and Apologizes for Injury Caused
In Love With Love	In Love With Another Person
Weakened by Time and Separation	Strengthened by Time and Separation
Wears off Over Time (The "I do's" become "you don'ts")	Lasts Forever ("I still do")

Society teaches us to love based on physical attractiveness, personality, prestige or some other temporary trait. This is dangerous because once these features fade or once something comes along that is more attractive, personable or prestigious, we soon lose interest.

True love is based on commitment and giving. It is a decision to serve and share your life with another person. John 3:16 tells us that "God so loved the world, that he gave his only begotten son, that whosoever believeth on him should not perish, but have everlasting life." This is the best example of perfect love. True love will give everything for the welfare of another. In a loving relationship, each person will do what is best for the other person even when it is inconvenient. For example, a woman was opening a bookstore and her boyfriend would go to the store to help her get things set up and helped with operations during the early days before she could afford to hire an employee. Another woman owns apartment buildings. Her boyfriend would do the lawn maintenance so that she would not have to pay someone to do something that he could do for her. When a man truly cares about a woman, this is how he treats her and vice versa. If a man is not willing to do anything to support you in your endeavors, as a popular book advertises, "he's just not that into you." Is he around when you need help or is he just around when it is time for fun? Is he only willing to help you if he gets something out of the deal? Is his radio station tuned to WIIFM (What's In It For Me)? Ladies, of course this works both ways. We should also be willing to help them without expectation of reward. When you love someone, you want to do things for them. It should make you happy to make them happy.

We live in a microwave society. Unlike a generation ago, we are used to getting everything quickly and without much effort. Concepts like sacrifice, selflessness and commitment are rarely discussed today. We are much less likely than our parents and grandparents to put forth the effort to make a relationship work. We are more interested in standing up for our rights than in working things out. We are more interested in our own immediate happiness and satisfaction than in the success of a relationship overall. Our motto usually is, "If things don't work out, I'm outta here." The attitude we should have is, "I don't care what it takes, I'm in there for the long haul." Two friends of mine dated when they were in college. They broke up and were best friends ever since. They are now engaged to be married some 20 years later. *His* motto has always been, "If my baby wants beef, some cows must die." Besides being funny, it demonstrates his commitment to her happiness. If both parties take that attitude a relationship is destined to work.

When the relationship is right, you have a commitment to each other, a determination to make things work even when trouble arises and a clear sense of who you both are. You are attracted to each others' strengths, but you realize that you have to live with each others' weaknesses. Some say that having a lot in common is important; others say that opposites attract. I say that there should be balance. Some couples are said to be "two peas in a pod." Having too much in common can be fun and comfortable in the beginning, but it may lead to problems in the long run. It is always enjoyable when you like the same foods, have hobbies in common, etc. But, if the commonalities are characteristics like procrastination, selfishness, poor communication skills, poor money management, etc., there will be big problems down the road. Likewise, some people say that differences keep a relationship interesting. Unfortunately, those very same differences that sparked your interest and seemed so exciting can cause friction in the long run. If you do not enjoy any of the same activities, if you have different lifestyle goals, different religious beliefs, etc, you may have a lot of friction as you try to relate to each other. The very habit that you thought "cute" in the beginning, can "get on your last nerve" in the end. A balanced relationship should have enough similarities to create a bond and enough differences to create energy. Thus, you get synergy.

It is also important to be trusting of each other and willing to show vulnerability. When that type of trust exists, people are willing to share their innermost thoughts and feelings. Listening is a key ingredient for nobody talks when nobody listens.

"Darcy" has been married for nine years. While that might not seem like a long time, she is still questioned by friends about how she and her husband are able to keep their marriage strong. They have dealt with blending a family, "baby's momma drama," etc, and have kept it all together. Darcy replies to her friends that she and her husband are very good friends who are able to talk about anything. She maintains that her secret is that she both loves and likes her husband–not always both at the same time, but at any time one or the other is present.

Ms. Door Mat, please realize that as much as you might want to be with Mr. Right Now, he will make that decision on his own. In conversations with girlfriends, we have come to the conclusion, and the Bible backs it up, that it is the man who does the choosing. "He who findeth a wife findeth a good thing." (Proverbs 18:22) Note that the verse did not say "she who findeth a husband." We are not supposed to be looking for them; they are supposed to look for us. Meanwhile, our task is to work on being that "good thing" that they will find. If a man is not interested in you, he just is not interested. You can cook, take care of his kids, buy him gifts, give him money, whatever you want, and he might allow you to do all of that. But, if he does not truly care about you, those things will not change his mind. So, we need to develop ourselves into the best person that we can be, with strong values that won't be shaken every time a handsome face with broad shoulders appears. When that happens, we will attract a quality man who will love us for exactly who we are–cooking or non-cooking, gift-buying or non gift-buying.

Ms. Door Prize, don't take this lesson too much to heart. This does not mean that you should not do nice things for a man you are dating, much less for your husband. It just means that the caring in the relationship is not based on that. The caring is based on character, values, commonalities, personality–both yours and his.

We must learn to consider the needs of others, not just our own. "Be ye likeminded, having the same love, being of one accord, of one mind. Let nothing be done through selfishness or conceit, but in lowliness of mind let each esteem others better than himself." (Phil. 2:2-3) If everyone applied this train of thought to relationships, there would be many more successful ones.

Door Hooks ¿

Do you believe that you understand the meaning of true love? How would you describe it manifesting itself?

_____

_____

_____

Does your current relationship (or past ones, if not currently in a relationship) embody the characteristics you described in your answer above? If not, what will you do to bring about the appropriate changes in order to have a loving relationship?

_____

_____

_____

If you find that your relationships do not meet your definition of "true love" … use the following affirmation or create one of your own: "In order to be the recipient of love from others, I must extend myself by showing love to others. My fulfillment is in the love that I give; it is not diminished if others choose not to accept the love I have to offer."

Chapter Fifteen

What It Means to be a "Help Meet"

God created Eve for Adam because it was "not good for man to be alone." Adam had dominion over all the earth–the animals, the fish, the land, the plants. He ruled everything, yet there was no one with whom he could communicate and have intimacy. Dogs make good pets, but try to have a meaningful conversation with one. The crops made for a good meal, but he had no one to look across the dinner table at.

Eve was created specifically to be a complement to Adam–a custom-designed companion–a role that no penguin, ostrich, elephant or emu could fulfill. Used in this manner, the word "meet" means "fit" or "appropriate." In other words, in Eve, God created the perfect companion for Adam. I Corinthians 11:8-12 states that the woman was created for the man, not the other way around. We are equal, but different. If we were both the same, one of us would be unnecessary. We serve complementary roles in each others' lives. For example, men base success on achievements, while women base success on relationships. Therefore, while both may have careers and both may perform household tasks, the man is more likely to be more focused on his career and the woman is more likely to be more focused on her family.

God chose neither the head nor the foot, but the rib, implying that man and woman are to be equal in their partnership and are to walk side by side through life. There is a poem of by Matthew Henry that goes like this:

Talayah G. Stovall

Eve was made by God
Not out of (Adam's) head to rule over him,
Nor out of his feet to be trampled upon by him,
But out of his side, to be equal to him
But under his arm to be protected and near his heart to be loved.

I have also seen the following verses inserted in the poem, but do not know their origin:

Not from the dust of the earth to compete with him,
Nor from his hand, that she should be his servant,
From his own rib–that he should love her as his own body.

The creation of woman also implies the importance of the distinction of the roles between man and woman. Man was made from the dirt. Woman was made from the man. While they are made of the same substance, flesh and bone, they were formed differently. Thus, man and woman form a partnership with distinct roles and characteristics.

Men and women are wired differently. Men are achievement-oriented. Women are relationship-oriented. That is just who we are. Although women are a major force in the job market, we still tend to put our careers in second place after our families.

The Hebrew word for "help meet" means "completer," "someone who assists another to reach fulfillment," or "help as his counterpart"–woman helps man by being his counterpart. The word is also used elsewhere in the Old Testament when referring to someone coming to rescue another. A help meet is a friend, an encourager, a supporter, a mood-lifter, a confidante. Because she was made from his rib, Adam referred to Eve, who he named Woman, as "bone of my bones and flesh of my flesh" Genesis 2:23. Note that Eve did not have to jump up and shout, "Hey, look at me!" Adam recognized her right away. Just as God brought Eve to Adam, He will present you to your man when you and he are both ready. God will put you in his path and he will recognize his "bone."

In the movie, "Rocky," Sylvester Stallone's character was asked why he loved his girlfriend, Adrienne, so much. His response was something like, "I dunno–I guess she fills the gaps." She was not the most beautiful or classy woman in the world and he was now on the road to riches. He could have had any number of women. But, there was something about her that he knew he needed. We are someone's missing "rib"–the one who will fill the gaps in his life, and our Adam will not be his best self until we are on the scene. Think about it, some poor guy is walking around in the world, not even knowing what is missing from his life. He feels a sense of discontent, but does not know why. He has the house, the car, a good career–but, something is still missing. Ladies, it is us! But, in order for the relationship to work as God intended, both the man and the woman must be ready.

The relationship you have with your spouse should supersede any other relationship that either has (other than your relationship with God). So, be sure that the man you are dating is one who you can put in that position. The proper relationship order is: God, spouse, children, job/church. As a single person, you are the queen of your castle and he is the king of his. It should remain that way after marriage. If one of you has children from a previous relationship, when you get married, neither should be demoted from that status. You are still the king and queen and that is your first responsibility. While you love and treat each other's children well, you should never give them the place that your spouse should have. A problem that often happens with families, especially when they are blended, is that one parent will go behind the other's back regarding the children. This should never happen. If you are not able to make that commitment, you should probably remain a single parent until your children are old enough for you to make that shift.

Both promise to love, honor and serve one another in poverty as in wealth, in sickness as in health, in joy and in sorrow, as long as they both shall live. There will definitely be problems in a relationship, but the vow is "until death do us part." This is a covenant that is meant to be kept for life, not just when things are running smoothly. Ironically, the word "covenant" and the word "convenient" only differ by a couple of letters, and one of those is "I." If we take the "I" out of it, stop focusing on what is best for us alone and focus on what is best for both parties in the relationship, there will be less emphasis on doing what is convenient for us and more emphasis on keeping the covenant the way God intended.

In order to determine whether you can make a commitment like this, you should ask yourself the following questions regarding the man of your desires:

- Do you like and respect him as well as love him? (Smokey Robinson sang "I don't like you, but I love you...") A lot of people end up married to people that they do not really like because they are infatuated and focused on surface characteristics rather than the deeper qualities a person possesses.
- Do you have frequent disagreements and arguments? If so, try to determine the source and resolve them right away. If they cannot be resolved, determine whether you are willing to live your life with constant discord.
- Can you both admit when you are wrong and apologize? It is important to be able to admit when wrong and to be willing to say, "I'm sorry." And mean it.
- Can you sit down and talk with each other easily?
- Do you have the same basic values? You do not have to be carbon copies of each other, but certain things like honesty, work ethic, etc. are important.
- Are there common goals that you can work together to fulfill? Your vocations are probably different, but you can still work together toward something, be it a house, your ideal retirement, etc.
- Do you trust each other?
- Are you supportive of each others' goals? If one partner's

goal would affect your overall lifestyle, how flexible will you both be? For example, what if one partner wants to leave his or her job to be an entrepreneur?

- Are you spiritually compatible? Do you have the same beliefs? Can you be tolerant of differing beliefs or is one partner expected to change? Can you pray together?
- Do you agree on how household chores should be handled? What are each person's expectations regarding meals, housecleaning, etc.?
- Do you have compatible decision-making styles? Similar styles can have positive or negative effects, depending on what they are. For example, if both are hasty decision-makers who make snap decisions or rash judgments, it could be very dangerous. At least one person should be level-headed. Or, if both are over-analytical, you can get caught up in the paralysis of analysis, where nothing ever gets done. Make sure that the styles work together.
- Would you be proud to introduce him to your friends, family and business associates? Would he represent you well or embarrass you?
- Are you physically attracted to each other?
- Is there an emotional connection and emotional balance in the relationship?
- Do you have any shared recreational interests/ common pursuits of pleasure? You don't have to like to do everything together, but you should like to do something together.
- Do you agree on whether outside activities should be participated in jointly, separately or a combination? Some couples like to do everything together, some like to have outside activities of their own. Either can work as long as both parties agree. The trouble occurs when one person wants to do everything together and one does not.
- Are you friends?
- Is there playfulness in the relationship? A sense of camaraderie?
- Do you have compatible social styles? Is one a

homebody while the other likes to go out all the time? Can you easily agree on where to go, what to do, etc.?

- How do both of you manage finances? Are the styles compatible? Is one or the other better at money management? If so, perhaps that person should take the lead in that part of the relationship.
- How do you manage conflict?
- Does he keep his promises?
- Do you have similar views on family structure? Do you agree on how children should be raised and whether one parent should stay home to raise them?
- Do you agree on how household responsibilities should be shared?
- Do you know what is important to each other?
- Would you like to be more like this person? Do you admire the traits that he exhibits? If you would not like to be *like* him, do you really want to be *with* him? This is not referring to things like biting his nails but to true character traits like kindness, honesty, etc. If he has character traits that you are uncomfortable with, perhaps you should examine your reasons for being attracted to him in the first place. If he has no traits that you admire, why are you with him at all?
- Does this person encourage and inspire you to be your best you? Are you both aware of each other's ultimate goals and desires? Are you each other's greatest cheerleader? You should be able to share the desires of your heart and know that he is not only supportive, but encouraging!

One of the relationships that I admire is that of one of my brothers and his wife. They know each others' faults (he is moody, she is a procrastinator...) and the differences they naturally have due to upbringing and life experiences. For example, one was brought up in a patriarchal family, the other a matriarchal one. They had totally different money management and bill paying styles. One was raised in the church and one was not. When conflict arises, one wants to talk while the other shuts down. While they acknowledge that there are issues, they also acknowledge the many traits in each other that are positive. They complement each other in many ways and both feel that despite their differences in style and personality, they would not trade each other for the world. I believe that my brother definitely found his missing "rib," his "bone." Like any couple, they had an adjustment period in the beginning and still work through the normal challenges, but even during those periods, they acknowledge how much they value each other.

They both tell the story of a time when they were extremely angry with each other about some issue and were not speaking to each other. My brother went to the garage to get the car out to go to church. Before he left, as his habit was, he also got the SUV out for my sister-in-law. He always did that so that she would not have to struggle with the baby and getting the car out of the garage. Of course, my sister-in-law was appreciative and very touched. When she saw him, she mentioned, "I was surprised that you still got the car out for me even though we are mad at each other." He replied, "Just because I am mad at you doesn't mean I don't love you." Needless to say, that argument was over. If you really love a person, you will demonstrate that love to them during the good times and the bad. You do not stop being nice to a person, and honoring them because things are not going well in the relationship at that particular time.

Door Hooks ¿

Is there typically a natural "fit" in your relationships or do you find that you try to force a relationship that is non-complementary to fit in order to maintain it?

How do you see yourself fulfilling the role of a "help meet"?

_____

_____

_____

If you find that you tend to "force" the fit in your relationships, use the following affirmation or create one of your own: "God designed me to be equal to but different from the man he intended for me. The qualities I have developed and am developing will be complementary to, and appreciated by, the man of God's choosing."

Chapter Sixteen

Wrapping Up (Hammering In the Nails)

A relationship can be likened to the human body. It is designed to work a certain way and to maintain optimum performance when we treat it the way it was intended. When we eat a healthy, balanced diet and get regular exercise, our bodies are fit and toned. But, sometimes, we tend to put things in it like rich sauces and fattening desserts–our bodies were not made to digest that stuff. As a result, they do not operate properly.

Likewise, if we do not have the proper ingredients to make a successful relationship, it will not operate in the proper manner. It may look good on the outside, but at its core, it is unhealthy. The necessary ingredients, like most good and healthy foods, are readily available, but are often more expensive than junk food. It is easier to maintain a surface relationship than to put in the real work that it takes to maintain a deep relationship. So, like with actual food, we ingest the cheap stuff–the fast food, which satisfies the taste buds temporarily–and avoid the healthy stuff. We settle for the short-term gratification of a "drive-thru" relationship, hoping that it will be good for us in the long run. But, sadly, while that milkshake and fries taste good going down, they do not provide the necessary nutrients to sustain us long term. While that man who looks good "on paper" might meet a short-term emotional need, he might not have the qualities necessary to sustain a long-term relationship. And, if you only focus on your own surface characteristics–

outward appearance and "pedigree"–you will not develop the inner qualities you need to be part of a healthy relationship.

In order to have the best, you must be your best. A man is not to wipe his feet on you, but neither are you to be his trophy. Becoming a "Door Belle" is a process; it requires deep introspective analysis of who you really are, and how you portray yourself. It requires an assessment of your weaknesses and your strengths, as well as recognition of what you really bring to the table. While many women and men concentrate on the good attributes they bring to a relationship, most have not been honest about the "junk" that needs fixing and discarding. Keep it real; do the hard work of looking in the mirror and seeing the authentic you, and be willing and determined to prepare your door to be opened to a relationship that is reflective of the evolution of your relationship with yourself and God...then you can cross the threshold to the love relationship you have desired, but never knew you could have.

Remember that while God is preparing you, He is also grooming your mate, so do not get ahead of His plan. And, when that man does appear, remember that if he is to be the head of your house, God should be the head of his life. If he does not allow God to lead him, he should not be leading you.

"Now unto to Him who is able to do exceeding abundantly more than we can ask or think, according to the power that works within us...."

God is ready to move you to the next level. Are you ready for the ride?

Door Hooks ¿

Are you using the proper ingredients to ensure a successful relationship? Or, are you in the relationship "drive-thru" lane?

_____

_____

_____

If your relationship "diet" is unhealthy, what changes will you make in order to optimize the performance of your relationships?

_____

_____

_____

If you find that you have been in "fast food" relationships, use the following affirmation or create one of your own: "I will slow down and reevaluate what I am putting into the body of my relationships. I will be sure to use the proper ingredients and to only become involved with others who are willing to make the same commitment to a healthy relationship."

Afterword

Messages on the Door

Ihope that reading this book has blessed you as much as writing it has blessed me. It was a journey at times. I wish you much success in all of your future relationships–romantic and otherwise. Here are just a few closing thoughts to bear in mind as you move through life:

"Belle-isms"

❖ You have special gifts and talents that God has given only to you. Focus on growing your gifts and living in your purpose.

❖ Do not be your own worst enemy. Stop sabotaging your progress by repeating the same mistakes over and over again.

❖ Take off that glass slipper, Cinderella, and put on a pair of work boots! There is much that can be done during your single years that will enhance your own life and benefit others. Think about how you can give back to society during this time.

❖ Lose that baggage! Ship it off to Tasmania or Timbuktu! Get it out of your life and get on with your life, totally free and clear.

❖ Never settle for less than you deserve–do not "cast your pearls before swine." (Matt. 7:6) You are a special lady and deserve to be treated as such.

- ❖ Focus on improving yourself first. Then, you will be ready for the man that God is preparing for you.

- ❖ We are all works in progress. God is not finished with any of us yet. No matter which "door" you have defined yourself to be, there is "Door Belle" potential inside of you. Plant the seed and grow it!

You are an "a'door'able" and exceptional woman! I expect to hear you ringin' and chimin' in the very near future!

About The Author

Talayah G. Stovall, a native and current resident of Chicago, IL, is an author, certified trainer and motivational speaker (CTM in Toastmasters, International), trained by "The Motivator,"

 Les Brown. She is the President of TGrace. Talayah believes in promoting a positive self-image and encouraging people to maximize their potential. She has an undergraduate degree in Business Administration with a Management concentration. After earning a Masters of Business Administration in Marketing from the University of Michigan, she spent 16 years in the banking industry before following her true passion of inspiring others through the written and spoken word.

Though she admits to having had a few "Door Prize tendencies" in the past, she is thoroughly committed to achieving "Door Belle" status. She is currently working on her next book, "Light Bulb Moments: Seeing God in Every Day Circumstances." Talayah is involved in a number of volunteer and professional organizations and has twice been recognized in "Outstanding Young Women of America."

Talayah G. Stovall

Collaborating Author

Rev. Valencia E. Edner is an ordained minister and Pastor of Collins Chapel CME Church, community college professor, musician and vocalist. A native of Detroit, Mi., she now resides

in the East Texas city of Lufkin. She has a M.S. from Southern ConnecticutState, and is currently working on an M.A. at Houston Graduate School of Theology. Formerly married but currently divorced, Rev. Edner knows first hand about the "perils of Door Mat living," and welcomes the opportunity to share the insights and wisdom of her experiences in order to make a difference in the lives of others.

To order additional copies of this book for your book club or church group, please visit our website:

http://www.talayahstovall.com

or email

talayah@talayahstovall.com

Both authors are available for speaking engagements.

This and other quality books are available from

OverLookedBooks

Visit us online at:
www.overlookedbooks.com